ASIAN AMERICANS

RECONCEPTUALIZING CULTURE, HISTORY, POLITICS

edited by

FRANKLIN NG
CALIFORNIA STATE UNIVERSITY,
FRESNO

A GARLAND SERIES

Asian Americans: Reconceptualizing
Culture, History, Politics
Franklin Ng, series editor

THE POLITICAL PARTICIPATION OF ASIAN AMERICANS

VOTING BEHAVIOR IN SOUTHERN CALIFORNIA

PEI-TE LIEN

Routledge
Taylor & Francis Group

LONDON AND NEW YORK

First published 1997
by Routledge
2 Park Square, Milton Park, Abingdon, Oxon OX14 4RN

Simultaneously published in the USA and Canada
by Routledge
711 Third Avenue, New York, NY 10017

Routledge is an imprint of the Taylor & Francis Group, an informa business

First issued in paperback 2016

Library of Congress Cataloging-in-Publication Data

Lien, Pei-te, 1957–
The political participation of Asian Americans : voting
behavior in Southern California / Pei-te Lien.
    p.   cm. — (Asian Americans)
Includes bibliographical references and index.
ISBN 0-8153-2984-9
    1. Asian Americans—California—Politics and government.
2. Asian Americans—California—Ethnic identity. 3. Asian Americans—California—Social conditions. 4. Voting—California.
5. Political participation—California. I. Title. II. Series.
E184.O6L54 1997
305.89507949—dc21

                                                              97-33628

ISBN: 9780815329848 (hbk)
ISBN: 9781138978805 (pbk)

Contents

Tables

Figures

Preface

Asians in America have had a long, though mostly subdued and unrecognized, tradition of political activism which did not come into public view until the student movement era of the late 1960s. Before protracted legal barriers to naturalization, immigration, and voting rights were removed bit by bit in the last half-century, political participation among Asians often assumed the more nebulous forms of civil disobedience, civil rights litigation, labor strikes, homeland independent movements, and wartime volunteerism. This polychromatic nature of the subject makes any attempt to study Asian American political participation parallel to the task of painting a chameleon. The outcome of the project depends much on the context of the investigation. Given different conceptions of the boundaries of "Asian America" and "political participation" and a separate time frame and method of data collection and analysis, one project may depart sharply from another in the scope and content of coverage and interpretation of results.

For instance, a project focusing on Asian American voting participation prior to World War II is most likely to be limited in scope and include only U.S.-born citizens of Japanese or Chinese origin who resided in Hawaii and did not become politically active until after the 1920s. Using the same time frame but focusing the research on non-electoral participation, the scope of participation may quickly germinate like seeds in a spring garden. The results may involve a much higher number of participants with various legal-political backgrounds (i.e., citizens and noncitizens, legal and illegal immigrants, foreign students, and visitors), broader ethnic origins (include Filipinos, Koreans, and Asian Indians), wider geographic boundaries (add Alaska and mainland states such as California, Illinois, Massachusetts, Mississippi, New Jersey,

Texas, and Washington), greater time span (can be dated back to the 1850s), and a more expansive list of political acts such as litigation, boycott, protest, strike, rioting, and provision of sanctuary and monetary aid to the political left of the homeland.

An ideal project of political participation focusing on the post-1965 era would include the electoral and non-electoral forms of activities mentioned above, but it could also include Asian participation in various post-Civil Rights social movements, homeland democratization movements, as well as other election-related arenas such as political contributions, campaign work, and community work. The geographic boundaries of ancestral origins would expand to include all areas of East, North, Southeast, and South Asia as well as the Pacific Islands. The pool of participants could reside in any one or more of the fifty states, but they could also come from anywhere outside of the United States proper. Lastly, immigrant-related issues such as adult resocialization, naturalization, refugee resettlement, access to social welfare, as well as voting rights-related issues such as redistricting, bilingual voting rights, and other electioneering techniques may become far more prominent than in the years prior to 1965.

In a nutshell, a project which attempts to include all aspects of contemporary political participation among Asians in America would be beyond the scope of a single volume work. It certainly is not the scope intended by this author. Instead, this project is based on rather narrow conceptions of political participation, population, and time frame. It focuses on the election-related participation of Asians residing in Southern California in the early 1990s. Fortunately or not, the study of Asian American political participation is such a neglected subject of research that even a small project like this can be considered to be pioneering in nature. I am both extremely excited by and apprehensive at this thought.

As a foreign student turned full-time homemaker turned part-time journalist turned political scientist, I did not become interested in the subject until I received my citizenship papers and realized that from then on, I too, could have a say in a government that I had been paying taxes to for many years. Like numerous new Americans born and raised in Asia, my joy over the acquisition of U.S. citizenship and the ability to register and vote was eclipsed by the internal battle between assimilation and ethnicity. I felt compelled to write a dissertation exploring this complex process of immigrant identification and political adaptation for individuals of my kind. Although the 1990 census indicates that every two out of three Asians were born outside of the U.S., their voices and concerns have too often been neglected by specialists in Asian American Studies. Moreover, in the discipline of political science, the scant attention paid to nonwhite ethnic minorities has been invested mostly on blacks and Latinos. The term "Asian" is hardly mentioned in any published work on the American electorate or mass political behavior. For these reasons, I chose to do a study focusing on Asian Americans but with a mainstream political science emphasis on electoral behavior and reliance on quantitative analysis of survey data. Through this effort, I hope to fill a research vacuum and to facilitate a dialogue long overdue between the two academic fields of study.

The selection of the research site of Southern California is partly a matter of fortuitous timing. At the time when I needed new datasets for analysis and failed to find money to create my own, the *Los Angeles Times* Poll happened to have completed several surveys with uncommon attention to Asians in Southern California. However, and more importantly, this geographical setting is unique in encompassing the largest Asian metropolitan area (Los Angeles-Long Beach) and is one of the most ethnically diverse regions of the nation. In the spring of 1992, it became the site of the most severe urban brawls in recent decades following the announcement of the non-guilty verdicts of four white policemen in the Rodney King beating trial. Naturally, Southern California should be on the top list of any scholars interested in the relationship between ethnicity and political participation in the early 1990s.

To project any sense of permanency on the political participation of Asian Americans from data collected at any one time-point and at any one site can be a highly treacherous endeavor. This is even more true of a study focusing on Asians in Southern California and in the early 1990s. This is a population and a community at the crossroads of fundamental structural and political changes. Among Asians, rapid sociodemographic changes since the 1980s can be illustrated by at least four population trends: continued multiplication of population, increased bipolarity in socioeconomic class, growing diversity in ethnic origin and birthplace, and escalated centrality of the foreign-born generation. The political implications of these trends are mixed. On the one hand, the sharp rise in overall group size may provide both a bargaining chip necessary for the decennial redistricting and a growing pool of political activists and candidates for public office. On the other hand, an increase in the number of prospective voters may be accompanied by growing divisions in political socialization, ideology, and partisan identification which in turn may hinder the bloc vote potential of Asians.

Significant changes external to the Asian American community have also taken place in Southern California over the last decade. These can be represented in such environmental changes as racial recomposition, economic fluctuation, resurgence of political conservatism, greater social inequality, and heightened racial tension, including an increased level of anti-Asian violence. Historically, anti-Asian sentiment has appeared in waves, reflecting changes in immigration patterns and economic conditions. Asians have been particularly vulnerable in recent times because of economic downturns, U.S.-Asia trade imbalance, media stereotyping, and rising population, among other factors. This sentiment culminated in the 1992 Riots when Asian small businesses, particularly those owned by Korean Americans, bore a disproportionate share of the losses inflicted by blacks and Latinos. The experience, nevertheless, also highlighted the perilous status of the "middleman minority" and provided a political rallying point for community organizations to mobilize citizenship application and voter registration. For some other Asians, the event was a wake-up call to challenge the marginalized status of the "model minority" and usher in an era of multiracial politics where the identification of collective interests among Asians is conducive to political participation and imperative to group empowerment.

A few years later, we learned that this anti-Asian sentiment was just a harbinger of the anti-immigrant and anti-minority sentiments that led voters in California to pass Proposition 187 (prohibiting illegal immigrants and their children from receiving social services) in 1994 and Proposition 209 (removing race, sex, ethnicity, and national origin concerns in the operation of public employment, education, or contracting) in 1996. In the nation's capital, the 104th Congress passed and President Clinton signed a welfare reform bill (Personal Responsibilities Act) in 1996 which was to deprive legal immigrants of social security benefits unless they belonged to certain exempt classes.

How have Asians responded to these challenges to the rights of immigrants and minorities in the last few years? Many community activists may contend that Asians have become politically mobilized by these situations. They can point to the large increase in the number of new citizenship applications and registered voters as well as the sizable proportion of foreign-born and/or first-time voters participating in the election exit polls conducted by a consortium of community organizations. Many may also mention the street demonstrations, campus strikes, voter registration drives, high-tech legislative campaigns, and information hearings organized and participated in by Asian Pacific Americans of all ethnicities, generations, ages, sexes, social strata, and geographic locations.

If these are all signs of a politically unified and activated community, then this glimmer of solidarity and empowerment is dimmed by the political money scandals involving John Huang and other immigrant Asians. Beginning in September 1996 with the *Los Angeles Times*' reporting of the Democratic National Committee's return of improper contributions solicited by Huang from a South Korean businessman, the mainstream media have engaged in a frenzied chase, following the convoluted trails of money from Indonesia, Hong Kong, Taiwan, Thailand, Guam, Pakistan, and China to the United States. Never before has news about political contributions made by or through Asians in America been covered so extensively and so negatively. Never before has Asian participation in mainstream politics been linked so closely to their homelands and their intentions questioned so much. For some Asians, this is another reason not to participate in politics. For others, this is a time to blame the immigrant entrepreneurs for not following the "American" rules. The majority of Asians in America are either uninterested or practically at a loss to respond. That is, until March 24, 1997, when racist portrayals of Asians reminiscent of the ones seen in the anti-Chinese era of the 19th century appeared on the cover of the news magazine, *National Review*. Many community advocacy organizations and professional and student groups seized the moment and publicly expressed their anger in protest.

Only time will tell if this series of events evolve into a period of crisis or opportunity for Asian American political participation. On the one hand, the campaign contribution controversy has created many casualties-- including John Huang and his like, political hopefuls, donors, and a political community further rifted by partisan, ideological, generational, and homeland political differences. These tend to weaken a community already short of political clout. On the other hand, the incident also illuminates the inter-connectedness of the United States and Asia as well as the growing importance of Asians in American politics. Moreover, the perception of institutionalized anti-Asian bashing at the national level may help to bring together political factions among Asians in the formation of a much needed strategic coalition. Thus, I think the outcome is still up for grabs and the interpretation of the impact is largely in the hands of Asians--in how they perceive the meaning of being Asian in American politics and in how they relate it to other movements in the social and political context. Whichever way it goes, the status of Asian American political participation is in flux and needs to be closely watched for a long while.

Acknowledgments

Being a "non-traditional" student and researcher in many senses, I am deeply indebted to my family as well as all the faculty members, office staff, colleagues, and friends in both Gainesville, Florida and Salt Lake City, Utah for their invaluable support. Over the years, each of these groups of individuals has come to my aid and contributed in various ways to the completion of this work.

My sincere appreciation goes first to my dissertation committee chairwoman, Professor M. Margaret Conway of Political Science at the University of Florida, who, despite many unanticipated professional and personal burdens, never turned down any of my numerous requests for advice and support throughout the years. I thank her for believing in my ability when I was doubtful; I thank her for listening when I was confused; and I thank her for being patient and understanding when my writing was awkward and my sentences cumbersome. For similar reasons, I am very grateful to other members of my dissertation committee: Dr. Wayne Francis, Dr. Michael Martinez, Dr. James Button, and Dr. Leonard Tipton. Without the constant guidance and encouragement from these professors, this book would not have been possible.

The Pacific Cultural Foundation of Taipei, Taiwan, deserves high praise for providing the money necessary to purchase books and equipment, analyze data, and present results at a national conference. Equally important, if not more so, are the Department of Political Science, Ethnic Studies Program, and the Research Committee at the University of Utah, which offered me ten weeks of release time and a research grant to conduct field interviews in Los Angeles and Washington, D.C.

Special thanks go to Dolores Jenkins, reference librarian and a dear friend at the University of Florida, for helping me locate and acquire useful survey data. I also want to thank Professor Don Nakanishi of the

UCLA Asian American Studies Center and to Rob Cioe, Jill Milburn, and Claudia Vaughn of the *Los Angeles Times* Poll for providing information on the datasets analyzed here.

My gratitude extends as well to those mothers and friends who sacrificed their leisure or otherwise productive time to volunteer in schools and on field trips so that I could go to school without much fear or guilt. Catherine Scott Freij of Salt Lake City, along with Kristi Long and Chuck Bartelt at Garland Publishing Inc. of New York, also command high respect from me for their hard work and unreserved support in the editing and production process. Without them, I could not have survived, and even enjoyed, the publication experience.

Last but not least, my deepest appreciation goes to my parents, my brother and his family, and my two darling children, Albert and Alice, for their unfailing faith, love, and understanding.

The Political Participation
of Asian Americans

CHAPTER 1

Introduction

THE CURRENT STATUS: A TWO-TIERED PICTURE

Although the first Asians arrived in present-day America long before the European immigrants,[1] Asian Pacific Americans (Asians, hereafter) have not been considered as a viable political force in the mainstream electoral politics until recent decades when changes in U. S. immigration policies and laws as well as economic, social, and political forces within and outside the United States converged to forge a new and accelerated era of Asian immigration (Daniels 1988; Takaki 1989; Chan 1991; Reimers 1992; Hing 1993; Ong, Bonacich, and Cheng 1994; Kitano and Daniels 1995). The 1990 Census provides some of the strongest evidence of the Asian emergence. The Asian and Pacific Islander population rose from 3.5 million to 7.3 million over the decade, with about 71% of the growth coming from immigration (U.S. Bureau of the Census 1993a). The Asian rate of increase of 108% between 1980 and 1990 was the fastest among all major U.S. groups. This rate was about twice that of Latinos, six times that of blacks, and 20 times that of non-Hispanic whites (U.S. Bureau of the Census 1993b). In five states (Hawaii, Maine, New Hampshire, North Dakota, and Vermont), the population of Asians equaled or outnumbered that of Latinos and blacks combined. It has been projected that if the current rate of growth holds—which is a likely scenario short of major changes in immigration policy and/or the global political economy—Asians will comprise about one-tenth of the nation's population by 2050 (Ong and Hee 1993).

In an electoral democracy where numbers count, this explosive increase in group size can be an indicator of the rising political power of Asian Americans. Moreover, the phenomenal growth of the Asian population has been accompanied by a remarkably high level of socioeconomic achievement in the aggregate. For instance, in March 1994, among persons aged 25 years old and over, the percentage of Asians with four or more years of college (41%) was almost twice the percentage of non-Hispanic whites (24%); their median family income of $49,510 among married couples was $4,270 higher than that of non-Hispanic white married couples in 1993 (U.S. Bureau of the Census 1995a).[2] Similar trends of Asian achievement were reported in a previous survey conducted in March 1991 (Bennett 1992). Most studies on American mass political participation often emphasize the defining impact of socioeconomic status—especially the role of education (e.g., Verba and Nie 1972; Milbrath and Goel 1977; Wolfinger and Rosenstone 1980; Conway 1991a). Judging from their high levels of education and family income, Americans of Asian origin would be expected to have high rates of participation in electoral politics.

In California, a state which accounts for 40% of the nation's Asian population, and particularly in Los Angeles County and its vicinity, home to the largest settlement of Asians in the mainland, the story of boom and prosperity is familiar. From 1980 to 1990, the state's Asian population grew from 1.3 million to 2.8 million with an increase rate of 128% (U.S. Bureau of the Census 1993c). It is projected that by 2020, Asians in California will number 8.5 million or about 20% of the state's population (Ong and Hee 1993). The percentage of persons aged 25 or over who had at least a bachelor's degree was higher for Asians (34%) than for non-Hispanic whites (28%) in 1990. The Asian median family income ($39,769) in 1989 was slightly higher than that for non-Hispanic whites ($39,032). In Los Angeles County, home to one-third of the state's Asian population, Asians again surpassed all whites in the percentage of those with higher education or family income.[3] And some have not been keeping the wealth just for themselves.

Journalistic accounts began to emerge in the mid-1980s on the disproportionate amount of campaign money donated by the Asian American community in relation to the size of the population. Lew (1987) observes that whereas Asian Americans constitute no more than one-tenth of the population in California, they often contribute 20-30% of the total campaign fund collected by a supported candidate. This figure can be much higher when the contributions are for Asian candidates. Tachibana (1986) reports, for example, that 75% of California's former Secretary of State March Fong Eu's campaign money and 70% of Delaware's former Lieutenant Governor S. B. Woo's fund-raising coffer came from Asian contributors. Formal and informal interviews conducted by the author in March-May 1996 with major Asian American elected officials and fund-raisers confirmed the continuation of this trend well into the 1990s.

Because of this demonstrated strength in campaign finance, both Asian and non-Asian political candidates now make special efforts to campaign in Asian American neighborhoods while highlighting Asian American concerns. Beyond state or local politics, Asian contributions made to national campaigns have been remarkable as well. Nakanishi (1997) reports that in the 1988 and 1992 national elections, Democratic and Republican presidential candidates shared about equally in the over $10 million dollars contributed by Asians. This makes the Asian American community second only to the American Jewish community in terms of the amount of campaign money raised by an ethnic minority group.

These figures help support the "model minority" thesis of Asian Americans established first by the mainstream media and picked up by politicians and the public in the wake of the Civil Rights Era, when the successes of Japanese and Chinese Americans were juxtaposed against the less advantaged situations of blacks and other minorities.[4] Yet the current status of Asian Americans is a controversial issue. There is no doubt that the legal status of Asians has drastically improved since the 19th century and the earlier part of the 20th century when formal and blatant discrimination and exploitation were the norm of practice (Chan 1991; Kim 1992; Almaguer 1994; Kim 1994; McClain 1994; Okihiro 1994; Salyer 1995; Kim 1996). Relative to other minority or even majority groups, Asians in the aggregate have clearly experienced a remarkable degree of economic success (Ong and Hee 1994). There is also little doubt that the election and appointment of Asians to federal, state, and local positions in recent years have become less novel. In fact, a review of the growing impact of Asians in American politics in terms of the number of elected and appointed officials in the last two decades identified a total of over 300 elected officials from 31 states and over 1,000 major appointees in 1996 alone (Nakanishi 1996). Today, in addition to their traditional presence in Hawaii,[5] Asians have become viable participants in many small mainland cities such as Fullerton, Monterey Park, Torrance, and Westminster in California, Mesa in Arizona, Fairview in Oklahoma, Carbondale in Illinois, Rochester in Minnesota, and, to a lesser extent, major urban areas such as Seattle, San Francisco, Houston, Omaha, Los Angeles, and New York.

If naturalization is an indicator of one's desire to become integrated into the American system, scholars concur that Asians in the aggregate have the strongest commitment to do so. In the last three decades, Asian immigrants petitioned to become U.S. citizens much sooner and at a higher rate than their counterparts from other areas of the world (Barkan 1983; Portes and Mozo 1985; Jasso and Rosenzweig 1990; Portes and Rumbaut 1990). However, a recent analysis of census samples finds that naturalization rates vary greatly across major Asian ethnic groups (Ong and Nakanishi 1996).[6] Among them, Japanese immigrants exhibited the lowest rates and Filipinos exhibited the highest rates of naturalization between 1970 and 1990. To speed up new citizens' process of involvement in electoral politics, a rising number of community organizations and major political parties have launched naturalization and voter registration drives and hired Asian recruiters in major urban areas in California, Illinois, New York, and Texas (Espiritu 1992; Nakanishi 1991; 1997).

In spite of the aforementioned indicators of progress, those who anticipate a corresponding growth of Asian participation in the American political power structure have so far been mostly disappointed. In terms of national office-holding, there have only been a handful of Asians—mainly Democrats, of Japanese descent, and from Hawaii or California—who have been elected to positions of power. Among the five voting members of Asian descent in the 105th Congress (1997-1999), for instance, four are Democrats, three are of Japanese ancestry, and two are from California.[7] Results of the 1990 Bureau of Census Civilian Labor Force data (Equal Employment Opportunity File) reveal that only 1.4% of all legislators surveyed in the nation were Asians.[8] At the local level, a 1987 Census of Governments reports that .07% of all elected officials nationwide were Asians (1988). This percentage rose to .13 when the same survey was administered in 1992; but it still compared poorly to the .42%

for American Indians, 1.4% for Hispanics, 2.7% for blacks, and 95.4% for non-Hispanic whites (1995b). Similarly, an analysis using the 1991 "Form of Government" Survey indicates that only .2% of the nation's city council members or mayors were of Asian ethnicity (MacManus and Bullock 1993). Federally appointed offices have also been inaccessible. In the early 1990s, only 45 of the 8,200 staff positions in Congress were held by Asians (Feagin and Feagin 1993).

In California, from the mid-1960s and throughout the 1970s, there were usually two or three Asians seated in the state legislature. However, there were no Asians seated in the state legislature during the entire decade of the 1980s, leaving Secretary of State March Fong Eu (1974-1994) the lone Asian in an elected position at the state level until the election of Nao Takasugi to the State Assembly in 1992.[9] Similar fluctuation exists at the local level. For instance, a Chinese American incumbent on the city council of Monterey Park (pop. 60,000, 57% Asian) was defeated in his re-election bid in April 1994, along with two other aspirants of Chinese origin, amidst reported fear of an Asian majority in the city council, where two of the five seats were filled by Asians in the preceding two years.[10] A few years earlier in 1986, the first Chinese American city councilmember (Lily Lee Chen) was removed from her office out of similar concerns over the rising Asian influence in the city (Fong 1994; Horton 1995). The city nicknamed the "first suburban Chinatown" has since been able to maintain only a single Asian councilmember (Judy Chu). In the early 1990s, in a state where one out of ten residents was Asian, only 2% of the state's top elected officials could claim their origin as Asian; only three out of the state's 53-member delegation to Congress were Asian; and only 1% of city council and school board seats were held by Asians (Efron 1990). Even the highest ratio of political representation found in the 1990 Census Equal Employment Opportunity File—i.e., 4.4% of all legislators in California were of Asian descent—pales when compared to the group's 9.6% share of population in the state.

The lack of elected or appointed Asian officials is mirrored by the low levels of voter registration and turnout by the American public of Asian origin. A 1984 analysis of voter registration lists for three areas of high Asian concentration in San Francisco reveals that people with Chinese and Japanese American surnames registered to vote at far lower levels (31% and 37%, respectively) than the 60% registration rate found among the general electorate (Din 1984). Similar findings are reported in a Los Angeles study where 43% of all Japanese were registered, followed by 36% of Chinese, 27% of Filipinos, 17% of Asian Indians, 13% of Koreans, and 4% of Vietnamese (Nakanishi 1986a). In the city of Monterey Park, Asian Americans' overall rate of registration was 29% in 1984 and 39% in 1989; the increase was mostly accounted for by new Chinese registrants (Nakanishi 1991). One consequence for ethnic empowerment was that in the municipal election of April 1990, non-Hispanic whites constituted the largest share of voters even though they were third in terms of population ranking (Horton 1995).

A statewide California ethnicity survey finds that Asians registered at 55% and voted at 48% in 1984; these rates are about 30% lower than those for non-Hispanic whites and blacks (Uhlaner, Cain, and Kiewiet 1989). In the June 1990 primary, the Asian registration rate of 39% was found to be the lowest among the four major groups in California (Field Institute 1990). In the 1992 presidential election, a *Los Angeles Times* exit poll indicates that the Asian percentage of the state-wide vote share was a dismal 3%, despite the group's 7% share of adult citizens. The situation appeared to be more of the same in the 1993 Los Angeles mayoral race where the Democratic candidate was an Asian (Michael Woo). Despite their 11% share of the city's voting-age population, Asians accounted for only 4% of the voters (Skelton 1993). Improved Asian vote share was reported by the *Los Angeles Times* exit poll for the 1996 presidential election, where 5% of voters identified themselves as Asians. Still, this represented only half of the percentage of adult Asians in the state.

Perhaps by far the most accurate estimate of Asian electoral participation rates is the Current Population Survey (CPS) series on the November elections since 1992 (Appendix A).[11] In 1992, of the sampled Asian population aged 18 or over in the United States, only 31% were registered to vote and 27% actually turned out at the polls. In 1994, the figures slid down to 29% for registration and 22% for voting. A major reason for the low level of participation may be that only about half of the Asian adult population are citizens. When citizenship status along with education and age are taken into account, Asian registration and voting rates increase substantially. However, there is still a 10-24% participation gap between Asians and whites.

Even in an area of American politics—donating money to political campaigns—where Asian participation in terms of the dollar amount given is not lacking, reactions to this emerging view of Asians as the "new moneybags" of American politics have not been entirely positive. From the Asian community's perspective, although they are known to contribute money in greater proportion than their share of the population, a big gap remains between what is promised and what is delivered to Asians—be it greater access to power or more high-level appointments that involve serious decision-making in government operations (Nakanishi 1991).[12] Moreover, the higher amount of money donated by Asians as a whole does not necessarily indicate that more Asians are involved in the political process. Comparing the extent of political participation between Japanese Americans in a California sample and the general population in a national sample, Fugita and O'Brien (1991) find that the rate of making donations among Japanese Americans is 26% higher than that of the general public. Yet, Uhlaner and her associates (1989) find that Asian respondents in California did not contribute money at a higher rate than their non-Hispanic white counterparts in the 1984 campaign.[13] In fact, those specializing in raising funds from the Asian American community observe both immigration generation and ethnic gaps in that the foreign-born tend to contribute in larger dollar amounts than the native-born. This is particularly true among the ethnic Chinese, Asian Indians, and Koreans. By contrast, some communities, such as Filipinos, Southeast Asians, and Pacific Islanders, tend not to be able to contribute in as great an amount, but they may often involve a greater number of contributors.[14]

From the opponents' perspective, much of the money donated to or by Asians is on a shaky legal ground, either because too much of it comes from outside of the district and/or because it may originate from somewhere in Asia.[15] Mainstream suspicion of illicit activities committed by Asians did not begin in the fall of 1996 or with John Huang, the first Asian American appointed by a major political party to a leadership position in charge of raising campaign funds from the Asian community.[16] Almost all successful Asian candidates—such as Congressman Jay Kim and former L.A. city councilmen Michael Woo and S.B. Woo, among many others—have been implicated at one time or another with receiving foreign or illegal campaign contributions.[17] However, nothing matches the scope of media and congressional scrutiny endured by John Huang and other Asian Americans close to the Clintons. This not only implies that some Asian Americans are perceived as approaching too eagerly and closely to the center of American politics, but that there is a long-term predicament awaiting Asians in terms of their need and ability to sever the homeland connections as well as to receive adequate recognition for campaign contributions made predominantly by foreign-born entrepreneurs.

In sum, although progress has been made over the years, observers note that "Asian American politics has remained to an unusual degree 'politics by other means,' i.e., not direct electoral representation but indirect access through campaign contributions, lobbying, litigation, and protest" (Erie and Brackman 1993, 47). Further, this "asymmetrical participation" through campaign contributions has not produced very efficacious results in terms of public office holding and political power. Instead, in the middle of 1997, it has brought harassment, shame, and anger to many long-term participants and community leaders (Wu 1997a; 1997b).

THE PUZZLE AND SOME MACRO ANSWERS

The preceding review of the current status of Asian Americans presents a two-tiered picture. Although the Asian American population has experienced an explosive increase in size and has enjoyed the highest levels of education, family income, and naturalization rates among ethnic groups in recent decades, the participation of Asian Americans either in government or in the electoral process has been extremely limited. Despite some evidence of an Asian gain in resources and leverage in recent years, the return in political representation is comparatively low and the community remains powerless to dodge or counter the attacks made by outsiders in terms of fund-raising scandals.[18]

Why is the political participation and representation of Asian Americans low in relation to their socioeconomic achievement and population share?

Numerous explanations, mostly at the aggregate level, have been proposed to explain the deficit. Some note the history of exclusion and discrimination experienced by Asian immigrants regardless of their national origins and time of arrival (Sandmeyer 1939; Daniels 1962; Saxton 1971; Daniels 1988; Takaki 1989; Chan 1991; Feagin and Feagin 1993; Hing 1993). A few mention the general antipathy toward government which is often an extension of the immigrants' unpleasant or frightening experiences dealing with corrupt regimes in their home countries (Nakanishi 1991; Skelton 1993), or the continued interference of homeland governments and politics in the Asian American community (Kim 1981; Kwong 1987; Chang 1988; Portes and Rumbaut 1990; Wang 1991).

Some emphasize the cultural impediment factor—that the Buddhist-Confucianist values of hierarchy, reverence for authority, resignation, and passivity are antidemocratic civic traditions discouraging Chinese, Japanese, and Korean Americans from participating in democratic partisan politics (Sue and Sue 1971; Kitano 1976; Jo 1984). Others attribute low participation to the legal restraints in the electoral system via the numerous practices of minority vote dilution. These include the requirements of geographic compactness and the bloc voting component in redistricting and in accessing a foreign language ballot (Bai 1991; Kwoh and Hui 1993; Ancheta and Imahara 1993). Still others mention the labor market segmentation which is responsible for the underemployment, underpayment, and a lack of upward occupational mobility of group members (Suzuki 1977; Cheng and Bonacich 1984; Kwong 1987; Light and Bonacich 1988). In his account of the Asian American Movement, Wei (1993) offers another set of reasons—the lack of a nationally known leadership, unified ideology, or even a plan of action.

Most basically, the participation potential of Asians may be severely discounted by certain demographic characteristics unique to an emergent multiethnic minority group. First, despite the rapid growth of the Asian American population in recent decades, the total number continues to be small and accounts for only 3% of the entire U.S. population.[19] Second, a large segment of the Asian American population is foreign-born, which means that they are likely to have limited proficiency in English and incomplete information about the political system and democratic processes, and would possibly not be eligible for citizenship and/or using the voting privilege for sometime (Rothenberg 1989). Third, the population is heavily concentrated in the Western region and mostly dispersed in a number of metropolitan areas where the cost of living tends to be higher and foreign-born immigrants and other racial/ethnic minority groups are also likely to congregate. Fourth, the population is fragmented across generations, ethnicities, nationalities, religions, languages, and social classes. In body politics, Asians are disadvantaged by their relatively small size, limited experiences, and tremendous internal diversity.

Yet, it remains unclear to what degree small population size and low population share impede Asian participation. For, unlike other minority groups, there exists a lack of correspondence between Asian American population size/share and political participation and representation. Asian Americans who have been elected often come from districts with a very small percentage of Asian population. A case in point is the 1985 election of Michael Woo to the Los Angeles City Council from a district that was only 5% Asian. Another example is the 1975 election of Norman Mineta to the U.S. House of Representatives from a district that was only 2.5% Asian. In the 1996 election, the first Asian American governor in a mainland state, Gary Locke, was elected in a state (Washington) with a 5% Asian population. On the other hand, municipalities having a high Asian concentration, such as Monterey Park and San Francisco, do not have a proportion of elected officials that comes close to resembling proportional representation.[20] In the same vein, Erie and Brackman (1993) find that homogeneous precincts with higher percentages of Asians do not have a larger turnout rate among Asians.

Many in the Asian community also contend that the image of socioeconomic success is more myth than reality, that economic deprivation, racism, and nativism persist, and that the gilded image only serves to increase the tension between Asians and other minority groups as well as among Asian ethnic groups (e.g., Suzuki 1977; Jo 1984; Hurh and Kim 1989; Lee 1989; Takaki 1989; Ong and Hee 1994; Espiritu and Ong 1994). They claim that the use of median family income and the like as indicators of wealth may inflate the value of income and mask the lack of economic participation of the group. A closer look into information presented in the March 1994 Current Population Survey (1995a) supports this assertion in several ways: (1) Asian families are larger in size. Seventy-three percent of Asian families consisted of three or more persons as compared to fifty-five percent for non-Hispanic whites in 1994.[21] (2) A higher proportion of Asian (62%) than non-Hispanic white (58%) householders worked year-round and full time. (3) Asians tend to reside in the West, in metropolitan areas, and particularly in central cities. In 1994, about six out of ten Asians resided in the West, almost all resided in metro areas, and about twice the proportion of Asians as non-Hispanic whites lived in central cities. (4) The profile of high educational achievement may not hold true for some Asian groups. Although fifty-eight percent of Asian Indians had at least a bachelor's degree, the proportion was much lower (6% or less) among Tongans, Cambodians, Laotians, and Hmongs.

As a consequence, the poverty rate for Asian families (14%) was almost twice as high as that for non-Hispanic white families (8%) in 1993 and the proportion of homeownership among Asians (52%) was lower than that among non-Hispanic whites (70%) in 1994.[22] Moreover, there is continued evidence of underemployment and lower educational returns. In 1994, the proportion of Asian males with four or more years of college in the executive, administrative, and managerial occupations (21%) was significantly smaller than that for their white counterparts (30%). Among college-educated women 25 years of age and over, similar proportions of Asians and non-Hispanic whites were employed in executive occupations, but a higher percentage of whites (49%) than Asians (36%) worked in professional occupations. The median earnings of full-time college-educated Asian male workers ($41,220) was lower than that for non-Hispanic whites ($47,180)—though both figures were much higher than the $32K earned by Asian or white women with comparable backgrounds. Perhaps because of the economic segmentation, past research has not been able to find a strong relationship between aggregated socioeconomic measures and voter registration (Nakanishi 1986a).

In sum, an overview of the existing literature using macro-level analyses suggests that the participation deficit of Asians may be attributed more to historical, cultural, homeland political, legal, economic, and group organizational factors, and less to objective socioeconomic class and demographic indicators. The puzzle lingers on: Are sociodemographic factors not useful in predicting Asian participation or are they less valid predictors for Asians than for other groups? Should we revise our understanding of the defining role of sociodemographic characteristics in political participation? What alternatives are there to predict the political participation of Asians?

AN ALTERNATIVE APPROACH: STUDYING THE INDIVIDUALS

Whereas each of these macro-level theories offers some insight into the roots of the Asian participation deficit, and the conceptualization of the current study certainly benefits from these predecessors, few give any estimate of the magnitude of the deficit as compared to other racial groups. No one has been able to compare in a systematic way the efficacy of one theory to another nor to explain individual differences in the extent and likelihood of participation. Without controlling for alternative explanations, association is often difficult to establish. And many, by focusing on structural constraints, seem to explain better the lack of, rather than the incidence of participation. Although qualitative data gathered by studies using in-depth interviews, participant-observation, community power, and ethnography provide great insight into the dynamics of participation in a designated setting, the narratives are limited to the context under study and cannot be used to make generalizations beyond the subjects chosen. Using the macro-level approach is therefore insufficient to answer the questions proposed above.

An individual-level, survey-based approach as adopted by this study, by contrast, is able to answer questions such as: Does being an Asian American matter for political participation? And how? What is the comparative role of socioeconomic status and other factors in linking group identity to participation for Asians and for other racial groups? What explains the participation patterns within the pan-Asian as well as specific Asian ethnic groups? These are questions raised by political participation research in the United States. Chapter 2 reviews five of the major theories of political participation in the discipline and evaluates the efficacy of each in studying Asian participation. Key concepts such as ethnicity and political participation are defined and hypotheses proposed.

One major reason past research has not focused on individuals is the lack of data, particularly large-scale comparative survey data. The one exception is the California Ethnicity Survey collected in 1984 by Uhlaner and others (1989) on which this author has conducted some re-analyses (Lien, 1992, 1993, 1994). In light of this research vacuum, a proposal to launch a large-scale in-language[23] national survey of Asians in America may be highly appealing. However, the complexities of sampling issues and interview costs involved are extremely high.[24] An alternative approach, secondary analysis of surveys previously collected for other uses, is therefore adopted by this study. An extensive search of major social science data archives and research institutes in the United States for opinion surveys with a significant number of Asian American respondents produced four polls collected by the *Los Angeles Times* in Southern California counties between 1989 and 1993. Two of them ("Asians in Southern California, 1993" and "Koreans in Los Angeles, 1992") are used in the analyses.

Chapter 3 describes the data sets used as well as the operational definitions of key concepts. Justifications and limitations of secondary analysis and of survey data are discussed. A methodological review on the studying of Asian American politics is also included. The results of the Southern California study are reported in Chapter 4. Additional methodological issues and results of the Korean study are the focus of Chapter 5.

Chapter 6 puts the question of a participation deficit in perspective by asking whether participation matters for Asians as a group and as compared to other racial/ethnic groups in the political environment. Differences between voter/participants and non-voter/non-participants in terms of sociodemographic outlook, minority group experiences, political information, policy preferences, and other political orientations are explored. Comparisons are also made between Asian and non-Asian voters in terms of the distributions and distances of their policy and political attitudes.

Chapter 7 concludes the study by revisiting the research questions and summarizing major findings. It then ponders the implications of the "non-significant" findings for models of Asian American political participation. Acknowledging the central role of the mobilization context, the study ends by discussing some of the movers and shakers in the ongoing Asian American Movement, namely political parties, ethnic community organizations, and the ethnic media.

NOTES

1. As early as 1565, Filipino sailors serving in the Spanish galleons jumped ship in Mexico and later made their way to the Louisiana seashores. These "Manilamen" created in 1763 the oldest continuous Asian American communities in North America (Espina 1988; Okihiro 1994).

2. The median family income of Asians in 1993 ($44,460) was also higher than that of the non-Hispanic whites ($41,110). However, the difference was not statistically significant.

3. The percentage of Asians aged 25 or older having four or more years of college education (37.2%) also exceeded that of non-Hispanic whites (30.5%). However, the median income for Asian families in 1989 ($39,296) was lower than that for non-Hispanic whites ($41,222).

4. The term first appeared in 1966. A *New York Times Magazine* article written by sociologist William Peterson compared Japanese American ascendance after WWII to the Horatio Alger stories. In the same year, *U.S. News and World Report* also printed an article celebrating the glowing success of Chinese Americans while condemning the failures of other minority groups. An analysis of media portrayals of Asian Americans in recent decades reveals some change of direction (Osajima 1988). Asian American issues of crime, school dropout, and poverty were gradually incorporated into the popular discourse in the 1980s. However, there have been continued emphasis on educational achievement and reliance on culturally-based explanations of success which tend to reinstate the "model minority" stereotype, neglect the social service needs of various Asian communities, and generate anti-Asian sentiment from other communities of color.

5. The political status of Asians in Hawaii is an exception. With Asians being the majority of the population, they have been active in local politics since the 1930s. A Chinese American, Hiram Fong, served as Speaker of the territorial House between 1949 and 1953. After statehood in 1959, Fong was elected to the U.S. Senate and Dan Inouye, a veteran of the highly decorated 442nd Regimental Combat Team, was elected to the U.S. House of Representatives from the territorial Senate. When Inouye won a seat in the U.S. Senate in 1962, his House seat was occupied by another Japanese American, Spark Matsunaga. The Hawaiian congressional delegation has been dominated by Japanese Americans, but the political power of other groups of Asians is also on the rise. For instance, in the 1994 mid-term election, a Filipino American, Ben Cayetano, was elected Governor by a population that was nearly two-thirds Asian.

6. Two limitations of using census data to estimate naturalization rates reported by researchers are: (1) The foreign-born population identified by the census includes nonimmigrants holding employment or student visas. (2) The data

only refer to the characteristics of the sample at the point of time when the information is collected (Ong and Nakanishi, 1996, 277).

7. The three Congresspersons of Japanese descent are: Senator Daniel Inouye (D-HI), Congresswoman Patsy Mink (D-HI), and Congressman Robert Matsui (D-CA). A fourth Congressman of Japanese descent, Norman Mineta (D-CA), quit Congress in October 1995. Besides Congressman Matsui, the second Asian delegate from California, Jay Kim, is a Korean American and a Republican,. There are also two nonvoting delegates in the House: Robert Underwood (D-Guam) and Eni Faleomavaega (D-American Samoa).

8. Because of the small population size, results on Asians from this government-sponsored survey or from any other public or private survey can only be treated as suggestive. Large-scale government surveys such as those reported in the Current Population Survey (CPS) have a much smaller sampling error than other surveys.

9. The absence of elected representatives did not necessarily mean that Asians were totally excluded from state politics. The Office of Asian/Pacific Affairs (1987-1991) created by former President Pro Tem David Roberti in the California Senate served, along with other Asian Pacific legislative aides, many of the same functions performed by black and Latino representatives for their ethnic constituents (Syer and Culver 1992).

10. Another reason for this as well as many other local defeats may be that having more than one Asian candidate running at the same time for the same office can split the community's votes and resources. Espiritu (1992) cites some instances of this in the city council elections in 1991. She perceives this to be a potential threat to the solidarity of the pan-Asian community.

11. Some cautions are necessary in using the census figures for estimates of voter registration and turnout. First, survey respondents tend to overreport turnout. For the 1992 election, the result is an overestimation of turnout by 9% in the census estimate (Jennings 1993). Second, racial minorities may have higher rates of overreporting (Abramson and Claggett 1991; 1992; but see Presser, Traugott, and Traugott 1990). Third, the sampling frame developed from the decennial Census and used by the Current Population Survey may have severely undercounted the nation's black, Latino, and Asian population (U.S. Bureau of the Census 1990; Leung and Mar 1991).

12. Part of the problem lies with the community's lack of experience in attaching a string to the opening of the "moneybag." An author comments that this may have started to change in recent years after a group of Chinese Americans formed a bipartisan Interim Coordinating Committee for Chinese Americans (ICCCA) to ask for better value for their money (Wei 1993).

13. The rates for Asians and non-Hispanic whites were 18% and 20%, respectively. The rate for Asian citizens was higher (24%). However, there were

ethnic differences in rates of participation in activities other than voting among the five major Asian groups surveyed.

14. These are from formal and informal interviews with John Huang, Lily Lee Chen, and many other Asian American community activists in the spring of 1996.

15. U.S. laws regulating federal elections currently permit contributions made by foreign-born legal residents and U.S. subsidiaries of foreign-owned companies that accrue profits from U.S. markets. However, federal campaign finance laws are elusive in defining what is "foreign" and are ineffective in preventing foreign money from being laundered into the U.S. system. Therefore, charges of Asian contributions being illegal are easier said than ascertained. Further, depending on local election laws, the receiving of out-of-district money under a certain amount may not be illegal at all.

16. John Huang's official title was Vice Chair of the Finance Committee of the Democratic National Committee in the 1996 Clinton/Gore re-election campaign.

17. From media accounts and personal interviews with each of the candidates in the spring of 1996. For a good journalistic account see Lim (1995).

18. An exception to this is the community reaction to the Chinese stereotypes appearing on the cover of the March 24, 1997 issue of the bi-weekly magazine *National Review*. Wu reports that major Asian American community and advocacy groups organized a media education campaign to teach the difference between Asian Americans and Asian foreigners (1997c). According to various media reports, community individuals and campus groups also protested vehemently against remarks made by John O'Sullivan, editor of the conservative magazine, who openly defended the editorial decision to use the racially offensive images.

19. According to the latest census report released in March 1997, Asian Pacific Americans were estimated to number 9.7 million in July 1996. Although this is a figure derived from samples, this number certainly represents a significant trend of population growth which keeps Asians as the fastest growing group of all major races in recent decades. Nevertheless, Asians still accounted for no more than 3.7% of the U.S. population in 1996 (U.S. Bureau of the Census 1997).

20. Although the Asian community has been a major presence in San Francisco since the 1850s, no Asian has ever been elected directly to the top governing body before November 1994. The deficit of political representation appeared to end in November 1996 when two more Asians joined Mabel Teng to serve on the 11-member Board of Supervisors.

21. An equal percentage (14%) of both Asian and non-Hispanic white families had three or more earners. This was different from 1989 when a higher percentage of Asian (19%) than white (14%) families had three or more earners (Bennett 1992).

22. Similarly, Bennett (1992) reports that the per capita income of Asians in 1989 ($13,815) was about $2,500 lower than that of non-Hispanic whites and a larger proportion of Asian individuals (14%) was below poverty, compared to that among non-Hispanic whites (9%).

23. Multi-lingual interviews conducted in the preferred languages of the respondents rather than in English are very much needed for an internally-diverse racial group with a large proportion of non-native English speakers.

24. None of the existing systematic survey sampling techniques can be satisfactorily applied to investigate the nationwide Asian population because of its extremely small size, geographic dispersion and sporadic concentration, ethnic diversity, and problems dealing with ethnic identification. According to an experienced Asian American pollster, the costs for bilingual-language interviews can easily double that of English-language interviews. The higher costs of the former are due to such factors as identification of Asian households in the sampling process, recruiting and training of bilingual personnel, and translation of the questionnaire into and from several major languages.

CHAPTER 2

Theories of Ethnicity and Political Participation

A number of theories exist in the current political science literature to explain the electoral participation of the American public in general (for recent reviews of dominant models, see Conway 1991b; Dennis 1991; Leighley 1995). Theories on the participation of racial/ethnic minority groups are few and often only refer to blacks (e.g., Verba and Nie 1972; Levy and Kramer 1973; Danigelis 1978; Ellison and Gay 1989; Bobo and Gilliam 1990; Tate 1993; Dawson 1994). However, an increasing amount of literature has emerged in recent years concerning Latinos (e.g., de la Garza 1987; de la Garza and DeSipio 1992; de la Garza, DeSipio, Garcia, Garcia, and Falcon, 1992; Hero 1992; de la Garza and DeSipio 1996; DeSipio 1996). By contrast, studies on Asians remain scarce (exceptions include Uhlaner, Cain, and Kiewiet 1989; Nakanishi 1986a; 1986b; 1991; Lien 1994; Tam 1995). In this chapter, five models of minority group political participation are discussed and their relevance to Asian Americans are examined. Special attention is paid to the concepts of ethnicity, panethnicity and the roles of socioeconomic status (SES) and socio-psychological factors in the shaping of political identity among Asian Americans.

DEFINITIONS OF KEY CONCEPTS

Before the relationship between ethnicity and political participation can be meaningfully discussed and analyzed, it is necessary to define the meanings of ethnicity, Asian American panethnicity, and political participation as adopted by this study. Perhaps because of the difficulty in drawing a clear conceptual fault line between race and ethnicity, these two broad terms have often been used interchangeably in the existing literature (Torres and Ngin 1995). Thus, a discussion of the meanings of ethnicity may include considerations of the role of race. Similarly, ethnic politics may be conceived of being no different than racial politics. This lack of distinction between race and ethnicity, though widely accepted, may become a source of confusion and friction when some ethnic group members are of nonwhite races or when a nonwhite racial group is composed of individuals with different ethnic and national origins. To help mitigate the problem, a third term, panethnicity, is adopted by this study as a special case of ethnicity to refer to the incidence of a collective group identity for a multiethnic, racialized group such as Asians.

Ethnicity

Ethnicity can be defined as a sense of belonging to "an involuntary group of people who share the same culture" or are perceived by others as sharing the same culture (Isajiw 1974, 122). Expressions of ethnicity for minority groups are complex and always occur against a backdrop of at least two levels of identification—with one's own ethnic group and with the dominant group (Yinger 1985; Hutnik 1986). For groups undergoing status change, the double boundary is often maintained from within by the socialization process and from without by the process of intergroup relations (Barth 1969; Isajiw 1974). For groups that have a recent history of international migration and are experiencing rapid changes in their population composition and socio-political position, the concept of culture, however, refers much less to an unmediated heritage than to socially constructed boundaries which can be created and re-created to organize group members (Roosens 1989). Immigrant group identity, therefore, is an "emergent phenomenon" rather than a static construct (Yancey, Ericksen, and Juliani 1976). Far from being an essence or something fixed, concrete, or objective, ethnic/racial identity is formed through the interaction between subjective identification and objective conditions and is constantly transformed by political conflicts (Omi and Winant 1986).

Ethnicity, nevertheless, may be derived not from one distinctive, integrated culture but from a multiplicity of cultures arbitrarily lumped together under one supranational group label, such as the inclusion of Mexicans, Cubans, and Colombians under the umbrella term, Latinos. These designations discount class, national, and generational cleavages. In these cases, the equivalent of the term "ethnicity," as it is used to classify individuals with Italian or Greek ancestry, then may be more appropriately called "panethnicity" or "the generalization of solidarity among ethnic subgroups" (Espiritu 1992, 6). According to Espiritu, previously unrelated and marginalized ethnic groups, thrown together at first by ignorant or insidious panethnic categorization and later by racial violence, may be able to confront the meanings of the imposed pan-group identity and the deprived group status by uniting together with each other to protect and promote collective interests. The result of this process—variously called "ethnicization" (Sarna 1978), "racialization" (Omi and Winant 1986), or "ethnic Americanization" (Fuchs 1990)—is the forging of a multi-tiered, situational, and partly ascribed panethnic culture. Although summarily called ethnicity in the existing literature, distinctions between panethnic or racialized group identity (panethnicity) and specific ethnic or nationality group identity (ethnicity) are often necessary and will be made throughout the book.

On the other hand, ethnicization is also a process of building up a sense of national identity with the host country (Garcia 1987; Finifter and Finifter 1989) where the extent of identification as being an American is at least as important as being an ethnic/racial minority. The term "assimilation" or the characterization of European immigrants' responses to the host environment, however, is highly inadequate to describe the process of becoming American for non-European immigrants (Feagin and Feagin 1993). Because of differences across immigrant groups in terms of peak time of entry, experiences of discrimination and stereotyping, availability of speedy and inexpensive transoceanic transportation and communication, and components in the political/economic structure such as the presence of urban political machines, many note that the assimilation experience of European immigrants cannot be transferred to immigrants from other parts of the world (e.g., Pachon 1985; Fuchs 1990; Hero 1992; Reimers 1992; DeSipio 1996).

Beginning with Gordon's (1964) notion that the adaptation of non-WASP (White-Anglo-Saxon-Protestants) may take place in a number of stages, many scholars perceive the Americanization of immigrants as an endless and dialectical process of acculturation (Parenti 1967; Hurh 1980; Keyes 1981; Padilla 1985; Keefe and Padilla 1987; Waters 1990; Kitano and Daniels 1995). During this process, immigrants may adopt certain cultural patterns in the public domain but maintain a distinct subculture in the private domain (Keefe and Padilla 1987; Hutchison 1988). They may also have any one of the four combinations of high/low ethnic identity and high/low acculturation levels (Hurh 1980; Kitano and Daniels 1995). The persistence of ethnic group culture, according to Portes and Rumbaut (1991), "has been the rule among immigrants, old and new, and represents simultaneously a central part of their process of political incorporation" (141). They may also become culturally but not psychologically or structurally adapted to their new national identity (Yinger 1985). Instead of predicting assimilation or the eventual adoption of a white American identity *and* the complete detachment from their ethnic culture over time, this multidimensional concept of ethnicity allows one the freedom to maintain ethnic loyalty at one level and to become acculturated to the new identity at another level.

Asian American Panethnicity

Although immigrant groups from different parts of Asia have a shared experience of discrimination and have long been labelled with racial terms such as "Asiatic," "Oriental," and "Mongolian," the development of an unified group identity or panethnicity among Asian Americans has a short history. The term "Asian American" was not invented and used until the late 1960s and early 1970s when U.S.-born college students, mainly of Chinese or Japanese origin, engaged in various protest activities on the West and East Coasts and in the Midwest (Umemoto 1989; Wei 1993). They were leaders of a Yellow Power Movement that came into being because of the convergence of at least three clusters of forces: (1) internal demographic changes within Asian America in the post-WWII era that resulted in the predominance of the English-speaking native-born population; (2) triumphs of the Black Civil Rights Movement and formations of other social movements such as Black Power, anti-Vietnam

War, New Left, and Women's Liberation Movements after 1965 which inspired the pursuit of group identity and rights among Asians; and (3) the emergence of pan-Asian organizations such as the Asian American Political Alliance and the publication of pan-Asian periodicals such as *Gidra, Getting Together,* and *Amerasia Journal,* which provided a common structure to facilitate communication and forge a pan-Asian group consciousness (Espiritu 1992).

A major achievement of the Movement was the installation of Asian American Studies on college campuses to teach the history of oppression and protest regarding Asians. Over time, followers of the Movement also helped the community obtain social justice and rights on numerous occasions, such as helping elderly Filipino tenants avoid eviction from the International Hotel in San Francisco, mobilizing the Chinese American community to fight for bilingual education rights in *Lau v. Nichols* (1974), and organizing a campaign to win the tenure fight of UCLA professor and community activist, Don Nakanishi, in the late 1980s (Omatsu 1990). Most importantly, the panethnic term has now been widely adopted by social service professionals and community activists, civil rights organizations, government agencies, and the mainstream media.

It would be a mistake, however, to characterize the Movement as enjoying wide-ranging, sustained success in reaching its immediate goal of creating Asian American courses on college campuses and the larger goals of racial equality, social justice, and political empowerment (Wei 1993). The success of the Movement has been mostly sporadic and limited by the changing political context, the group image of assimilation and success, the internal divisions among participants in geographic region, ideology, class, gender, and strategy, and the lack of national organization and leadership (Jensen and Abeyta 1987; Wei; Espiritu and Ong 1994). Besides, despite the institutionalization of the inclusive panethnic label, Asians in America seldom think of themselves as a single people. They often identify themselves as being from a certain Asian country or even a certain district or region within a country. In times of ethnic exclusion and persecution, they have also practiced "ethnic disidentification" for self-protection and survival (Espiritu 1992, 20-4).

Given the list of external and internal constraints, pan-Asianism can be identified as an ideology primarily endorsed by U.S.-born and U.S.-educated middle-class Asians. If conceived solely based on sociodemographics, the constituency for panethnicity in the 1990s is extremely small compared to the majority of the population that is foreign-born. Nevertheless, as detailed earlier, the construction of a group culture is often not voluntary and self-identification with a racial or ethnic group based on primordial ties may not be sufficient to index the feelings of attachment or concerns over group interests. Instead, because of the drastic political and social changes within and outside of Asian America in the last three decades, the origin of a racial or ethnic group identity may be increasingly dictated by situational, contextual forces rather than by primordial ties. Further, evidence of (pan)ethnicity may best be revealed by multiple indicators measuring such dimensions as acculturation, ethnic attachment, and group consciousness. More discussion on the layers of ethnicity can be found in Chapter 3 which delineates operational definitions. Suffice it to say that at least when the right context emerges, e.g., the prevalence of racial violence, the urgent need for social service funding, or the need to overcome the arbitrary and inconsistent census classification of persons of Asian origin, pan-Asian group consciousness can be raised and political action mobilized (Espiritu 1992).

Political Participation

Scholars disagree on the meaning of "political participation" (Conway 1991b). In the first chapter, political participation was defined as including not only actions by individuals to influence the selection and/or the actions of government officials (Verba and Nie 1972) but also the outcome of this participation in the sharing of governing. The purpose for doing so is to give a more comprehensive picture of the political status of Asian Americans—the distance between political actions and the goal of full empowerment. For the individual-level analysis that is the main thrust of this study, the definition offered by Milbrath and Goel (1977) that covers individual actions and/or attitudes both to influence and to *support* government and politics seems to be a more appropriate means for describing the participation process for recent immigrants. Examples of participation used by the surveys include citizenship intent and naturalization for the foreign-born, voter registration and voting for citizens, and for all members of the society, making campaign contributions, contacting officials, attending political meetings or fund-raisers, and volunteering for a political cause.

Some studies have found political participation to be multidimensional (Verba and Nie 1972; Milbrath and Goel 1977; Bobo and Gilliam 1990). Because of the differing degrees of information and motivation required for each type of activity, those who vote often do not necessarily share the same level of involvement as those who join with a group or organization to solve community problems, work for political campaigns, or contact elected officials. However, some note that, at least in the past twenty years, participants tend to overlap in activities that require the same kinds of resources, but not to the extent of clustering in identifiable "modes" (Rosenstone and Hansen 1993). This is supported by a study on Asian and Mexican Americans where voting and other conventional activities can all be loaded into one factor (Lien 1994). Thus, the dimensionality of participation remains an open question.

Voting is often observed to be a blunt indicator of the overall satisfaction and involvement of the public. However, it also provides an equality no other types of participation can afford: each citizen gets one and only one vote (Verba et al. 1993a). For the majority of Americans, voting requires few resources (registration and information) and is easily practiced (Teixeira 1992). Yet, for people of color, the promise of voting equality did not begin to take shape until the passage of the Voting Rights Act of 1965. The opportunity for political equality for nonwhite and non-English-speaking individuals did not arrive until the passage of an amendment in 1975 that permitted the use of bilingual ballots and a second amendment in 1992 that mandated bilingual voting materials be made available in jurisdictions that reach a 5% threshold OR with at least 10,000 voting-age, single language, limited English proficiency citizens (Kwoh and Hui 1993). Before the installment of these legal guarantees, citizens of Asian origin, like citizens of African or Hispanic origins, had to overcome the barriers of English-only elections, literacy tests, racial gerrymandering, and physical intimidation and violence to register to vote (Wei 1993). For new immigrants, there is an additional "cost" to this most common form of participation—the acquisition of citizenship, which is itself a process most likely to be influenced by proximity to the mother country, fear of officials from Immigration and Naturalization Service, lack of information and knowledge, difficulty in meeting language and civics requirements, and a general lack of a sense of political efficacy and trust rooted in the political institutions of the mother country where socialization was initiated (Fuchs 1990). Other barriers that increase the cost of participation for recent immigrant groups include the regionally-dispersed and geographically-concentrated distribution of the population and the high proportions of the young and the new, along with the institutionalized practices of minority vote dilution (Pachon 1985). Many of these and other determinants of participation are discussed in the next section.

MODELS OF MINORITY GROUP POLITICAL PARTICIPATION

Group Culture Model

To explain the distinctive patterns of political participation of racial/ethnic minorities, a common approach in survey-based research is to attribute the patterns to a composite group culture variable as denoted by one's self- identified or ascribed race, language, religion, or national origin. Assessment of the independent impact of the ethnic factor is then achieved by adding some control over a respondent's socio-political background. Although this approach is useful in capturing whatever group-related effect is left unexplained by other quantifiable measures in the equation, this cultural definition of group identity has increasingly been criticized in recent years for being reductionist and not reflecting the evolving or situational nature of ethnicity (Patterson 1975).

Nonetheless, as discussed above, the meaning of culture for any ethnic or panethnic minority group includes more than primordial ties. The supranational group label "Asian Americans" was not created spontaneously by persons of different Asian ethnic group origins. Instead, it was the product of the interaction of external and internal forces that helped to create and re-create the political community. To the extent that an Asian American culture exists, it is most likely to appear in a multifaceted and transient format. Perhaps because of this unique property of ethnicity, a past attempt by Uhlaner et al. (1989) achieves little in terms of locating a universal principle that can account for the participation of

Asians as well as for that of blacks, Latinos, and non-Hispanic whites. It is possible that for Asians, the meaning of "culture" for political participation may have an entirely different ramification than that for whites, and that differences between the two groups cannot be explained away by sociodemographic background and group consciousness. It is also possible that existing measures of participation, which often focus on one's experience in the United States, may fail to fully account for the transnational and cross-cultural experience of Asians in America (Lien 1994).

This study, which focuses on the election-related participation of Asians in Southern California, hypothesizes that, to the extent that Asian Americans can be treated as belonging to one composite group culture, they may be associated with less participation. The size of the participation deficit may vary, however, according to one's sociodemographic background and political attitudes structuring one's ethnicity. Within each Asian ethnic/nationality group, the role of ethnic group culture in political participation may be similar to that for the pan-Asian group.[1]

Socioeconomic Model

The defining impact of socioeconomic indicators—especially education—has been well-established in the American political participation literature (e.g., Verba and Nie 1972; Milbrath and Goel 1977; Wolfinger and Rosenstone 1980; Conway 1991a; Leighley and Nagler 1992a; Verba, Schlozman, Brady, and Nie 1993b). Evidence generally supports the idea that citizens of higher social and economic status participate more in electoral politics. This may be partly attributed to the comparative lack of political cleavage along class lines in the U.S. two-party system (Verba, Nie, and Kim 1978). Education, too, may impart democratic values and information about government and politics, nurture a sense of competency and efficacy that predisposes an individual to political involvement, and provide facilitating skills to obtain more information about politics. Income, on the other hand, may enable the disposal and conversion of wealth into other resources or the trade-off for other opportunities and reduce the costs of participation (Rosenstone and Hansen 1993). Education, in addition, can increase one's opportunity to be placed in social networks through employment, organization membership, and volunteer work (Verba et al. 1993b). Given that this conclusion is often derived from observing the white majority, it remains to be seen if it can be applied to different nonwhite ethnic groups in America.

When socioeconomic factors are added to assess the independent impact of ethnicity, many studies find that the difference in voting and registration rates between blacks (or Latinos) and whites decrease or disappear completely (e.g., Milbrath and Goel 1977; Conway 1991a; Teixeira 1992; Verba et al. 1993b). This indicates that the impact of class may be more important than ethnicity. However, given the empirical relationship between socioeconomic class and ethnicity, the impact of class may be overemphasized and the role of ethnicity underplayed. Nelson (1979) studies the relationship between class and ethnicity by examining behaviors of five ethnic groups in New York. He finds support for the hypothesis that ethnicity has an independent influence on participation over and above socioeconomic class.

Classifying persons of Hispanic origin into three nationality groups, Calvo and Rosenstone (1989) show that the education-turnout relationship holds for Mexicans and Puerto Ricans, but not for Cubans. Higher educated Cubans do not turn out more than their coethnics with a grammar school or lower education. Similarly, studies on Asians using either an aggregated or individual approach find a lack of relationship between socioeconomic class status (SES) and registration or turnout (Nakanishi 1986a; Lien 1992). By comparison, Lien (1994) finds that Mexican Americans in the same survey displayed a very strong relationship between SES and participation in voting and other types of activities. Because a larger proportion of both Asians and Cubans have a higher SES than Mexicans and Puerto Ricans, it is possible that SES may have a stronger impact on structuring participation among the lower status groups.

Yet, it may also be possible that the influence of socioeconomic factors on participation may be *weaker* for emergent minority groups such as Asians and Latinos *than* for the more established groups such as non-Hispanic whites and blacks. In the same study by Calvo and Rosenstone (1989), the impact of education and income is less significant for Hispanics than for non-Hispanics. The reason for this may be that persons of Hispanic origin may find it harder to translate their educational achievement into resources for participation (i.e., information, time, and money) either because of language difficulty for the foreign-born,[2] lower returns for educational attainment in income and employment, or because of the many compelling demands on immigrant group members in their daily struggles to adapt to their adopted land. Second, past socialization either in an undemocratic homeland or in a democracy with blatant legal discrimination against newcomers may impede the development of political efficacy and a sense of civic duty that are found to increase participation. Third, the emergent minority status of the group and the lack of perceived benefits (via representation in government) may negatively affect the participation potential for both U.S.-born and foreign-born members.

Demographic Model

In addition to socioeconomic factors, demographic factors specific to the immigrant population such as nativity, age, length of stay, and gender may have a substantial impact on participation.[3] These factors are particularly important for studying the participation of new immigrant groups, for these are the factors that may have direct or indirect bearing on the extent of social learning and integration. As one ages or stays longer in the adopted land, one may acquire language skills, know more about the host community, produce a second or more generation, become eligible for citizenship, and develop political interests in the adopted society because of the many stakes involved.

Converse (1969) comments that sheer time or the passage of years in chronological age only serves as a proxy for how much exposure an individual has in the political environment. He notes that for foreign-born immigrants, the length of stay may be a better indicator of exposure to U.S. politics than age. Lee (1980) observes that being foreign- born may imply a lack of experience with the American political system, preoccupation with economic survival, interference from the home government, an unawareness of the need to assimilate, weak organization membership, cultural ambivalence, and a fear of social rejection by the mainstream. However, when length of stay (or age for the native-born) or percentage of lifetime spent in the United States (length/age) is used along with nativity, other studies find them to be less useful than age in predicting participation (Uhlaner et al. 1989; Uhlaner 1991; Lien 1994). Gitelman's (1982) study on the resocialization of Russian immigrants into Israeli society also notes a lack of linear relationship between length of stay and political adaptation except in the early years of arrival.

Part of the reason for these counterintuitive findings may be that, like the political learning of young adults (Jennings 1989), there is a certain formative period in the immigrant's life history when loyalty to a new political system can be imprinted. This threshold effect appears to be at work in Black, Neimi, and Powell's (1987) finding of a positive relationship between age and the acquisition of partisanship and other indicators of political involvement among *new* immigrants to Canada.[4] More basically, much of the relationship between time and participation is made under the assumption that there is an upward social mobility over time. Although Dahl's (1961) assimilation theory that the importance of ethnicity will succumb to class concerns has been seriously attacked for its lack of validity (Parenti 1967), his assertion of a positive association between social mobility and time in the host nation—particularly over generations of immigration—has not been seriously challenged.

As a matter of fact, demographic factors, like socioeconomic factors, have received substantial support from studying Latinos because of the relatively larger presence of the young, the new, and the poor among the immigrant population (e.g., de la Garza 1987; Calvo and Rosenstone 1989; Fuchs 1990; Hero 1992; Garcia, Garcia, de la Garza, and Falcon 1992).[5] Many Asians are also younger in age and newer to the country than the white majority, but they are not necessarily poorer or undereducated. It is, therefore, hypothesized that demographic variables will not have as strong an association with political participation among Asians as among other racial groups. Further, other conditions being equal, age may be more useful than other indicators of time to predict Asian participation. Yet, among the foreign-born generation, length of stay may be the most important correlate of participation.

Gender. The role of gender in nonwhite ethnic group political participation has been controversial because of the implied conflicts between feminism and cultural nationalism. Critics in both the Chicano and Asian American Movements have worried that an emphasis on women's identity and rights would divide the ethnic community in its struggle against racism (Chow 1987; Garcia 1989). Yet, research using either an individual or a community-based approach has not provided much support for the hypothesis that feminism hurts racial minority group empowerment. Being nonwhite and female is often not a liability in political participation.

Perhaps boosted by being conscious of the "dual oppression" of both sexism and racism, black women typically participate at higher levels than their male counterparts (Verba and Nie 1972; Shingles 1981; Baxter and Lansing 1983; Jennings 1993). Although black females were more likely to be partisan, show interest in political campaigns, and register to vote than black males in the 1984 election, the gender advantage of black female participants disappeared when factors such as income, home ownership, and political interest were controlled (Tate 1993). The observations on Latinas are a bit more complex. In the first national survey of Latinos, being a woman of Mexican or Cuban origin was an insignificant predictor of turnout but being a woman of Puerto Rican origin depressed the turnout in 1988 (Garcia et al. 1992). For Californians with Mexican or Asian ancestry in the election of 1984, gender was an insignificant predictor of voting or other types of electoral participation when sociodemographic and attitudinal factors were controlled (Lien 1994).

Support for the role of gender in motivating ethnic political participation is more evident from recent community studies. In a study of the Latino community in Boston where Puerto Ricans constitute a substantial portion of the population, Latina women are found to make up the majority of the participants and activists at all types of political events (Hardy-Fanta 1993). Similarly, Saito (1992) observes that Asian women are involved in politics at all levels and their success as candidates and community activists has been crucial to constructing the Asian political base in Monterey Park, CA. This is so despite the consistent findings from census studies that more Asian American women are compelled to involve themselves full-time in the labor force and receive lower returns for their education than do white women (Matthaei and Amott 1990; Chan, 1991; Bennett 1992; Kim and Lewis 1994). A rationale behind the phenomenon is that, like the Latinas in Pardo's (1990) study, the dual obligation to the family and work place may facilitate the development of social networks and transform the concern over education and other family issues into more involvement with community issues and political action. This, in turn, may compensate for the socialization bias that encourages submission and passivity. The net effect in terms of mass politics may be the insignificance of gender in participation.[6]

The role of gender in mobilizing Asian participation can take a downward turn when it intersects with nativity. For many, especially non-English speaking, foreign-born Asian women, the potential for political participation can at least be triply depressed by prior socialization that did not treat women as equal partners, by their new obligation to join the immigrant labor market for economic survival, and by the need to adjust to being members of an American ethnic minority. It is, therefore, hypothesized that although gender may not be significant in and of itself, being a foreign-born Asian woman may depress the likelihood of participation in the U.S. political system.

Socio-Psychological Model

The role of socio-psychological factors such as partisan attachment, sense of civic duty, political efficacy, interest in politics, trust in government, and concern over election outcome has asserted its importance on participation studies ever since the seminal work by Campbell and his associates (1960). In terms of comparing participation across ethnic groups, Verba and Nie (1972) introduce the concept of group consciousness which was found to compensate for the disadvantaged SES of blacks in the late 1960s. Later scholars find that black group consciousness matters because of its linkage to political efficacy and trust (Shingles 1981). Extending the examination to cover members of both subordinate and dominant groups, Miller and his associates (1981) emphasize that it is the interaction of group identification and politicized consciousness that mobilizes participation. Adopting the concept of Miller et al., Uhlaner and her associates (1989) find that group consciousness can help explain away the participation disparity between non-Hispanic whites and Latinos but not between non-Hispanic whites and Asians. Lien's follow-up study (1994) finds that for both Asian and Mexican Americans in California, the concept of group consciousness is multidimensional, with each dimension having different ramifications for voting and other types of participation for each of the two immigrant groups. She finds that the addition of racial alienation and deprivation indicators, along with other indicators of the ethnicization process such as acculturation and ethnic ties, improves our understanding of participation for both minority groups.

In light of the strong empirical support for socio-psychological factors, it is likely that a similar multifaceted nature of ethnicity can be found in this study. It is hypothesized that measures indexing the shaping of ethnic/racial group consciousness and identity in America such as personal experiences of discrimination, concern over group status and interests, and attitudes or efforts supporting integration/acculturation may be associated positively with participation, whereas indicators of ethnic resilience may not be associated negatively with participation.

Legal Constraints Model

In contrast to conventional legal models that deal with the differences in registration requirements across the American states (Wolfinger and Rosenstone 1980; Caldeira, Patterson, and Markko 1985; Calvert and Gilchrist 1993; Rosenstone and Hansen 1993), this discussion of immigrant group participation examines the effect of two legal prerequisites for enfranchisement, citizenship status and voter registration.[7] Prior to the 1950s, Asians' lack of participation in electoral politics can mostly be attributed to the discriminatory immigration and naturalization laws and other legal restraints at federal, state, and local levels. Among the more infamous were the Nationality Act of 1870, Page Act of 1875, Chinese Exclusion Act of 1882, Alien Land Laws of 1913, Asiatic Exclusion Act of 1917, National Quota Act of 1924, Tydings-McDuffe Act of 1934, and Executive Order 9066 which authorized the internment of Americans of Japanese origin on the West Coast between 1942 and 1945 (Chan 1991; Kim 1992; Hing 1993; Kim 1994; Salyer 1995; Kim 1996).[8]

In California, between 1879 and 1952, the state constitution prohibited employment of the Chinese by any government entity or corporation in the state. Earlier, between 1854 and 1872, a Chinese individual could not testify against whites. Antimiscegenation laws prohibiting marriage between Asians and whites were not removed from

California statutes until 1959. Until 1943, the Chinese were categorically denied immigration to the United States and citizenship was not accessible to those already immigrated into the country. Immigration and naturalization for Asian Indians and Filipinos were not possible until 1946 and for the Japanese and Koreans not until the passage of the McCarran-Walter Act in 1952. But the number of individuals eligible for this process was still severely limited by the racist quota system implemented by the 1924 Immigration Act. The United States did not lift most of the restrictions on Asian immigration until the passage of the Immigration and Naturalization Act of 1965.

Today, citizenship status is granted automatically to all those born in this country and it is one of the prerequisites for voting. Those born outside of the United States, who want to be politically empowered by being able to vote, must first go through a lengthy and complicated (and often costly) process of naturalization. It requires legal residence of five or more years with at least thirty months of continuous physical presence in the United States prior to filing the petition, a record of good moral character, and successful completion of exams on the English language and U.S. history and government.[9] Cleared of these and other legal barriers, it still is a decision which depends on the joint operation of at least three sets of factors: individual characteristics, conditions of the homeland country, and the perceived benefits of U.S. citizenship (Jasso and Rosenzweig 1990). For instance, immigrants may not wish to pursue U.S. citizenship if they do not consider the ability to sponsor the immigration of relatives, to obtain jobs, to register and vote, and, after 1996, to receive social welfare benefits[10] as important. Some may not wish to acquire U.S. citizenship because of the reluctance to explicitly repudiate allegiance to their countries of origin and the privileges attached to holders of non-U.S. citizenship.

If speedy naturalization is an indicator of one's desire to become integrated, then Asians in the aggregate have the strongest commitment to stay and be incorporated into U.S. society. Barkan (1983) finds that between 1958 and 1978, despite great variations among nationality groups, eight out of ten foreign-born Asians were naturalized by the eighth year of residence; comparatively, the ratio for non-Asians was five and a half out of ten. He thinks that a major reason for Asians' exceptional speed may be their greater employment of early naturalization. From 1976 to

1986, Portes and Rambaut (1990) report that the naturalization rate of Asians was six times that of Mexicans. But they also note great variations among the Asian nationality groups, particularly that between Vietnamese and Japanese immigrants.

In an examination of the pattern of naturalization for immigrants from twenty-three countries in the 1970s, Portes and Mozo (1985) make a similar observation and explain that the high rate of Asian naturalization may be related to the lack of geographic proximity to the homeland, the more political than economic motive of emigration, and the higher educational and/or occupational backgrounds. Jasso and Rosenzweig (1990) suspect that a major driving force for speedy naturalization may be the ability of U.S. citizens to sponsor family members to immigrate to the United States. In contrast, Pachon (1991) notes that Latino immigrants have the highest incidence of noncitizenship because of a general confusion over the real benefits of citizenship and the process for attaining it. Although political participation other than voting does not require citizenship status, it is likely that those who make the effort to become eligible to vote or are born eligible to participate in basic politics will also be more attuned to participating in political activities other than voting. Yet, judging from the non-political motivation of recent non-refugee immigrants from Asia, a more likely scenario is that citizenship status may not have much relationship with participation likelihood (Erie and Brackman 1993).

Once naturalized, immigrants still need to face another hurdle before they are able to vote in elections. Today, voter registration may be considered a relatively simple procedure of filling out a brief form which is now widely available in many public places because of the Motor Voter Act. Even so, registration can be discouraged by the 30-day residency requirement and the need to re-register after moving to a different jurisdiction, or to file for a change of address if moving within the same city or county. Before 1965, African American citizens (particularly those residing in the South) were hindered from registering because of discriminatory attitudes and procedures such as literacy tests, all-white primaries, poll taxes, harassment, and violence (Conway 1991a). For citizens with a non-English background and/or those who did not immigrate until adulthood, the likelihood of registering can be further hindered by cultural passivity,[11] ignorance about the proper procedures, the lack of foreign-language forms and other election materials,[12] fear of election officials, and a general lack of a sense of efficacy in the abilities of government to solve problems.

The registration requirement, therefore, can be a major barrier to voting for immigrant groups. In fact, some suggest that registration can be more difficult than voting (Rosenstone and Wolfinger 1978). In addition, past studies have shown that like voting, registration has a class bias; among those who move, re-registration is less likely for those who have lower levels of education or political interests (Squire, Wolfinger, and Glass 1987). Because registration costs are part of the costs for voting, it is hypothesized that registration levels may be determined by similar factors that predict voting. Moreover, because registration may signify more than a basic interest in politics, being registered to vote may have a spillover impact on the probability and extent of participation in other kinds of election-related activities.

SUMMARY

Two key concepts of this study—ethnicity and political participation—are conceptually defined in this chapter. The five sets of factors previously found to influence minority group political participation—ethnic group culture, socioeconomic status, demographic background, socio-psychological attitudes, and legal constraints—are discussed. These five models by no means exhaust the possible explanations for political participation. Many studies, for instance, emphasize the importance of strategic mobilization by political elites in a campaign environment (e.g., Patterson and Caldeira 1983; Caldeira, Patterson, and Markko 1985; Cox and Munger 1989; Uhlaner 1989; Leighley and Nagler 1992b; Rosenstone and Hansen 1993; Jackson 1996). Some find prior socialization or behavior to be crucial (Marquette, Green, and Wattier 1991). These five sets of theories are proposed because they are theoretically important and available for empirical testing using available datasets (which are discussed in the next chapter). Also, because each model of participation can only be thought of as being one small cog in a gigantic machine, the efficacy of each may be best tested when others are controlled. Multiple regression analysis, a statistical method designed for such a purpose, and other methodological issues are discussed in the next chapter.

NOTES

1. An unfortunate difficulty in the author's past and present query into the internal diversity among Asian Americans is that the sample size for each ethnic group is far from satisfactory. It ranges from n=50 for Filipinos to n=89 for Koreans in the 1984 survey and n=23 for Koreans to n=57 for Japanese in the 1993 survey. Results on the role of specific Asian ethnicity are therefore only indicative of its impact. However, our understanding of the role of ethnic identity in the shaping of Asian immigrant political integration may be improved by focusing on the experience of one of the groups. Results from a large-scale survey of Koreans in Los Angeles (n=750) are reported in Chapter 5.

2. In the census publication on the foreign-born population in 1990 (1993a), about half of the Asian immigrants reported that they could not speak English well (49.9%) and about one-third reported living in a linguistically isolated household (30.3%).

3. Citizenship status is also a very important factor. However, for the purpose of analysis, this will be discussed under the legal constraints model.

4. Alternatively, threshold effect or period effect may be involved. The effect of time may also be curvilinear, but we do not have longitudinal data involving Asians to test these hypotheses.

5. Yet, support for the influence of demographic variables was in fact mixed in the Latino National Political Survey (Garcia et al. 1992). Whereas immigration generation had a positive effect on the Mexican and Puerto Rican American turnout in 1988, the impact of age was insignificant when other factors were held constant. And neither immigration nor age could predict turnout for Cuban Americans.

6. Part of the reason for the lack of effect may be that many individual level studies do not control for working women outside the home, who may be more likely to participate than those who work at home.

7. This legal constraints model is excluded in the analyses of Koreans because no voting turnout data are available for them.

8. References for the next paragraph also come from the same resources.

9. Important exceptions to this set of rules such as the reducing or waiving of residency requirements to spouses of U.S. citizens, spouses of certain U.S. citizens stationed abroad, children adopted by U.S. citizens, or to military personnel serving in the U.S. armed forces may be particularly beneficial for certain groups of immigrants to expedite the naturalization process.

10. Because of welfare reform laws passed by the 104th Congress in 1996, legal US. residents will lose Medicaid and other social security benefits unless they are refugees, asylees, parolees, veterans and members of the Armed services

and their families, persons for whom deportation is being withheld, or permanent residents with 40 quarters of covered work under the Social Security Act.

11. The primacy of the cultural factor has been seriously challenged by some recent scholars of Àsian American and Latino politics.

12. Although Asians are a federally-designated minority and are protected by the foreign-language provision of the 1975 Voting Rights amendment, the law is more discriminatory to Asians because of the multilingual and residentially-dispersed characteristics of the population. A recent change of threshold criterion to include any jurisdiction with 10,000 or more single-language and English-deficient citizens is expected to alleviate some of the problems.

CHAPTER 3

Methodology

STUDYING ASIAN AMERICAN POLITICAL PARTICIPATION

A study of Asian American political participation can mean different things to different people. This is because there are many facets to Asian Americans' history of involvement in U.S. and homeland politics (Parrillo 1982; Chan 1991; Lee 1996). The scope of a project hinges on a number of elements, such as time frame of analysis, research methodology, and definitions of geographic boundaries, ethnic identities, and political acts. However, because of protracted legal barriers to immigration, citizenship, and voting participation, the participation of Asians in mainland electoral politics did not begin to assume a more publicly visible scale until after the 1960s.

In a sweeping review of research dealing with Asian American politics, Nakanishi (1986a) distinguishes between electoral and non-electoral participation. Within the non-electoral arena, he also separates domestic from transnational issues and acts. Although the boundaries of research seem endless, he notes that "[w]hat exists is largely confined to descriptive and historical inquiries" (p. 2) which can be broken down into four areas: (1) discriminatory political actors and policies in U.S. society and system; (2) responses by Asian immigrants to both discrimination in the United States and events in their homelands; (3) case studies of the actions of Asian Americans; and (4) community and organizational studies exploring the internal dynamics among competing groups. Nearly absent from this literature, observes Nakanishi, is quantitative analysis that utilizes voting and registration data. As indicated in the first chapter, even the very small number of researchers that collect quantitative data often discuss results at the aggregate level.

One can think of at least four explanations for this highly skewed phenomenon in the conduct of inquiry. First, the history of Asian involvement in U.S. mass-based politics is very brief. Large-scale participation in elections was not possible until layers of legal barriers to voting participation were removed and the size of the population was allowed to multiply. In mainland politics, this meant a delayed start in participation until after the 1960s. Second, the utmost mission of Asian American Studies has been to construct a group history of one's own. This preoccupation with history is natural, given the pervasive scope of omission and distortion of Asians in America and the relatively young age of the discipline. Third, the enormous pressure to achieve success under the model minority stereotype may lure away those quantitatively-oriented Asian students and scholars from investing more in humanities and social sciences. Lastly, researchers submitting proposals for collecting quantitative data on the political participation of Asian Americans may receive less favorable reviews because of the perceptions that either Asians are insignificant in American politics or they are not a disadvantaged group in need of research support or both.[1]

The lack of attention and research on Asian American electoral politics appears to have changed somewhat since the 1980s because of a rapidly growing Asian population and a concurrent rise in the number of Asian candidates in local and state politics on the West Coast. Following a slow but steady flow of journalistic reports, mostly in the ethnic media, with occasional reports from the mainstream media,[2] topics of Asian American politics have started to attract interest from academia, government, and the non-profit sectors in recent years. Fifteen years after the publication of the first anthology on Asian American political participation (Jo 1980), there have emerged at least six theses or dissertations (Din 1984; Jun 1984; Ger 1985; Saito 1992; Lai 1994; Lien 1995), a few specially-commissioned reports (e.g., Cain and Kiewiet 1986; Nakanishi 1986b; Muratsuchi 1991; Ong, Espiritu, and Azores 1991; Erie and Brackman 1993; Shinagawa 1995), and a number of single-authored or edited book chapters (e.g., chapter 9 of Chan 1991; chapter 9 of Fugita and O'Brien 1991; Nakanishi 1991; chapter 3 of Espiritu 1992; chapter 5 of Hing 1993; chapter 8 of Wei 1993; chapter 7 of Fong 1994; chapter 8 of Ong, Bonacich, and Cheng 1994) on the subject of mainland electoral politics. A book-length manuscript on multiethnic politics in Monterey Park, CA, hit the shelf in 1995 (Horton). Relatedly, an edited book focusing on community activism across the nation debuted in 1994 (Aguilar-San Juan). Finally, a professional journal *Asian American Policy Review* began its annual publication in 1990 to complement the distinguished but interdisciplinary *Amerasia Journal* (1971-).

THE NEED FOR SURVEY DATA

Despite recent growth in research interest, studies adopting a micro-level approach for analyzing Asian American participatory behavior are rare. The main obstacle is the lack of large-scale survey data. To this author's knowledge, only one set of survey data (Cain and Kiewiet 1986; Uhlaner et al. 1989) was available during the entire 1980s for systematic examinations of participation differences across Asian and other minority groups. Perhaps because of the emphasis on the comparative perspective of ethnic political participation, this highly valuable data set omits a number of items that may be of specific concern to the immigrant community (Lien 1994). The reliance on the regional telephone directory of one nationality group (*1984 Korean Telephone Directory of Southern California*) to yield more than one-fourth of the state's Asian sample is also a source of potential bias. Further, given the volatile nature of multiethnic politics in the 1990s, the information revealed by the survey needs to be updated.

The problem with the lack of data is acute and may be difficult to overcome without substantial research support and ingenuity in design. Owing to the panethnic group's small population size, ethnic-lingual diversity, and the extremely dispersed residential pattern, it is tremendously challenging to design a survey that is both cost-efficient and representative even for a limited geographic area. This means that in virtually every multiracial-group survey, Asian respondents, if identified at all, are often scarce in number and their opinions tend to be underrepresented and/or misrepresented. One example of this was in the California statewide exit polls conducted by the Field Institute in 1992. Of the 8,170 questioned, less than 300 were Asians. Even in a huge national-level survey such as the ABC/CNN exit polls conducted during the 1992 general election (N=15,490), only 156 Asians were included.[3] Similarly, of the over 16,000 participants in exit polls conducted by the Voter News Service (VNS) for the 1996 election, only 170 were Asians. A severe consequence of this systematic underrepresentation is the potential distortion of Asian opinion. VNS initially reported that 43% of Asians voted for Clinton. It later issued a corrected estimate of 53%—which was about the same as the Clinton vote among Asians in Southern California, but it was 8% less than the one in Los Angeles County and 18% less than the one in New York City. The Asian figures were reported by a consortium of Asian community organizations who conducted their own multi-language exit polls in many locations of high Asian concentration in California and New York.[4] Their data portrays the Asian vote in a different light than mainstream organizations.

In designing surveys that focus on Asian Americans, scholars need to make tough choices balancing the demands for efficiency and coverage; either can be very costly if the size of the sample is also a concern. Yet, the cost of not having more individual level data on political participation may be even higher. We will not be able to know, for instance—

What is the likelihood that an Asian American will register and actually vote in elections? What factors—be they social class, level of educational attainment, ethnicity, generation, sex, occupation, or religion—have the greatest influence on an individual's likelihood to register, affiliate with a specific party, or become involved in other activities, such as contributing campaign funds, or seeking public office? Which issues are most likely to gain Asian American voters? (Nakanishi 1986a, 6)

These are explanatory questions about electoral reality to which "[s]urveys, with all of their limitations, constitute the most direct, and thus most valid, way of finding answers" (Dennis 1991, 52).

LIMITATIONS OF SECONDARY SURVEY ANALYSIS

A compromise between the need for collecting survey data and the lofty costs involved in data collection is secondary analysis. Although this research method is increasingly popular, particularly in times of economic fluctuations, secondary survey analysis sometimes is impossible because of the unavailability of data, the mismatch between primary and secondary objectives, the unduly long delivery time, poor data quality, errors made in the original survey, and—as illustrated above—when the number of cases in a specific subpopulation is too small to conduct the desired statistical analysis (Kiecolt and Nathan 1985). In addition, the problems intrinsic to the survey method are applicable to the secondary analysis as well. According to Babbie (1989), one of the complaints of the survey approach is that it can fragment the complexities of life into discrete, clean-cut, and unitary variables. The other is that it is superficial and seldom deals with the context of social life. Surveys cannot measure social action—they can only relay self-reports of recalled, hypothetical, or prospective action. Surveys may also suffer from a lack of validity because of the need for standardization. Fortunately, some of the problems associated with surveys can be allayed through sophisticated statistical analyses. For this project, the author was able to skirt some of the problems dealing with secondary analysis through the acquisition of two Southern California surveys conducted by the *Los Angeles Times Poll* in 1992 and 1993.

DATA

One of the data sets on which this study is based was drawn from an August 1993 *Los Angeles Times* (LAT) survey of adults residing in the following six counties in Southern California: Los Angeles, Orange, San Diego, San Bernadino, Riverside, and Ventura. Random-digit dialing techniques were used to produce the base sample. Asians and African Americans were oversampled to ensure a large enough number of respondents for analysis by targeting telephone exchanges with high black or Asian density levels.[5] The margin of sampling error for the total sample is plus or minus three percent. The margin of error for Asians is plus or minus eight percent. Telephone interviews were completed with 221 Asians, 199 Latinos, 144 blacks, and 646 (non-Hispanic) whites.[6] The interviews were conducted in English and Spanish. About half (55%) of the entire sample and three-fourths (72%) of the Asian sample were from the Los Angeles city and county area.

Compared to the 1990 Census, the proportion of Los Angeles County residents in the six-county area was about the same as in the LAT sample (52%), but the proportion of Asians in the sample was 10% higher than that in the census (62%). As is expected with any survey data, respondents' levels of education, income, and the extent of political participation (citizenship, registration, and voting) were higher and the share of foreign-born was lower than in the census (Appendix B). However, the share of high family income in the Southern California sample was about the same as in the census of Los Angeles County; and the rate of voting among citizens was only slightly higher in the Southern California sample than that in the national sample reported by the Bureau of the Census.

A second data set used by the study was drawn from a LAT survey of adult Korean residents of Los Angeles County between February 26 and March 27, 1992. Random-digit dialing techniques were again used to produce about one-third of the sample; the rest were drawn from lists of Korean-surnamed households countywide. Telephone interviews using Korean (93%) and English were completed with 750 Koreans. Translation and interviewing were conducted by Interviewing Services of America. The margin of error for the sample is plus or minus five percent.

Compared to information provided by the 1990 census, the sample was overrepresented by those having higher education, but is equally represented in terms of the proportions of higher income families, naturalized citizens, and (among those aged 24-64) those who were foreign-born. The sample percentage of the college-educated (49%) was 15% higher than what was reported in the census among those age 25 or older in 1990. However, in a pattern consistent with the Asian data mentioned above, the share of high income families (50k or more) in the Korean sample (31%) was about the same as that in the census (29%). So were the proportions of adult foreign-borns (99%) and naturalized citizens (36%) among survey respondents.

Although the two LAT polls are area surveys, they are preferable to previously collected data of a similar nature in that a popular variant of probability sampling technique—random-digit dialing—was incorporated. This may increase the generalizability of results and lower the size of errors from sampling and other sources.[7] Another advantage of the polls is that they contain a fairly large amount of information on race/ethnic relations and other political attitudes. This unique information provides contextual background to the key concepts investigated in this study. One of the drawbacks of using the two polls, as is true with any secondary analysis, is the lack of a perfect match between vital research topics and surveyed items. For example, omitted in the polls are direct measures of subjective group identification as well as political party affiliation and pre-immigration political socialization. Examining only the Southern Californian communities also impairs the generalizability of results to other parts of the nation. This may be a significant limitation of the study. However, the extent of bias regarding Asians is hard to estimate because of the lack of comparative data from other communities.

METHOD

The goal of this study is to understand the meaning of being Asian in political participation. This is approached by exploring the relationship between ethnic identity and political participation at several levels. At the panethnic group level, Asians are compared to blacks, Latinos, and whites. Among Asians, the Chinese are compared to Japanese, Koreans, Filipinos, and the Vietnamese. Among Koreans, the structure and influence of a specific Asian ethnicity is compared to those conceived at the pan-Asian level. Hypotheses derived from the five participation models discussed in Chapter 2 are tested to find out whether Asian group identity matters, how it matters, and what accounts for the incidence of participation among Asians in general and Koreans in particular.

In the process, three levels of analysis are involved. At the univariate level, the operational definitions of dependent variables and independent variables are introduced and a discussion of their frequency distributions follows. At the bivariate level, the zero-order relationship of participation indicators to basic sociodemographic and socio-psychological factors are discussed. At the multivariate level, the relative importance of various explanations for ethnic political participation hypothesized earlier are examined. Separate analysis is run for respondents of all racial groups and for the Asian group.

For the Southern California data, logistic regression, a statistical method for handling dichotomous dependent variables, is used to analyze the likelihood of citizenship/naturalization, registration, voting, and participation in any one of the other political activities. Multiple regression procedure is used to analyze the extent of participation in activities other than voting. For the Korean data, because of the absence of voting and other participation indicators and the presence of a fuller range of ethnicity indicators, attention is paid to the development of ethnicity and its causal influence on naturalization, citizenship intent, and voter registration.

OPERATIONAL DEFINITIONS

Political participation

As indicated in Chapter 2, the definition of political participation in this study refers to the conventional, election-related activities that private persons use to show their allegiance to the political system. Examples of such activities in both data sets include naturalization for the foreign-born and voter registration for citizens. For the Southern California sample, participation activities also include citizen voting, and for all members of the society, making campaign contributions, contacting officials, attending political meetings or fund-raisers, and volunteering for political causes. For the Korean sample, the intent to become naturalized is conceived to be another indicator of participation. Question wording for political participation and other variables is reported in Appendix D.

Because the Southern California data include an extensive list of participation items used by previous scholars to simulate the structure of participation (e.g., Verba and Nie 1972; Milbrath and Goel 1977; Bobo and Gilliam 1990), several principal component analyses using varimax rotation were conducted to determine the dimensionality of participation for this sample. The results for the full sample consisted of all four groups of respondents and the subsample of Asian respondents indicate that those who register and vote are not necessarily more likely to participate in other types of activities. On the other hand, those who contact officials are more likely to contribute money, attend political functions, or volunteer for a political cause.[8] A summed index of participation other than voting was created by taking the summed score of the four items of participation mentioned above. In addition, a dummy indicator of participation was also calculated by assigning a value of 1 to those who indicated their participation in any of the four activities.

For the Korean immigrants in Los Angeles, their level of incorporation into the American political system may be conceived as being comprised of an ascending order of citizenship intent, citizenship, and voter registration, with each succeeding act demanding more of the newcomers than the previous one. Because of the non-conflictive nature of these participation items, the term "political integration" is sometimes used to refer to the participation of Koreans in later chapters. Principal component results using varimax rotation indicate that the three acts could all be loaded into one dimension.[9] A four-point scale of participation was created by assigning a value of 3 to those who registered to vote, a value of 2 to those who were naturalized but not registered, a value of 1 to those who were not naturalized but expected to become so in the next few years, and a value of 0 to those who had done nothing.

(Pan)ethnicity—Function of objective background

For the Southern California data, a respondent's cultural background is measured by his/her answer to the question about racial origin. Dummy variables for black, Latino, and Asian group identity are created to allow comparisons with the impact of being white. For Asians, a respondent's ethnic group background is determined by his/her response to the question about country of origin. Examination of the effect of ethnicity among Asians is conducted by first limiting the respondents to those belonging to the five major nationality groups in the sample and then creating dummy variables for each of five groups except for the Chinese.

(Pan)ethnicity—Function of subjective factors

In concluding her widely-acclaimed book on the institutional aspect of Asian American panethnicity, Espiritu (1992, 168) remarks that "[a]n important next step would be to quantify this consciousness by studying interpersonal pan-Asian ethnicity—most important, its marriage patterns." Although intermarriage is the most studied form of assimilation/ adaptation, Williams and Ortega (1990) summarize six other types of indicators based on Gordon's theory (1964; 1978): culture (language, cultural practices); primary-group structure (neighborhood, friendship, organization membership); ethnic group identification (importance of ethnic background); attitude reception (perceived prejudice); behavior reception (experience of discrimination); and issue opinion (conformity to the majority opinion). In studying Asian participation, there is an urgent need for not only a formal measure of the state of panethnic group consciousness, but multiple measures of the possible sources of fusion (English proficiency, common experiences of prejudice and discrimination, organizational influence, i.e., exposure to ethnic/nonethnic media, affiliation with political parties and other social organizations) and fission (attachment to ethnic group culture, concern for homeland politics, etc.).

The two data sets do not contain a direct measure of (pan)ethnicity, but they do contain a high number of socio-psychological factors relating to the construction of (pan)ethnicity. For the Southern California sample, possible indicators of ethnicization include those approximating the extent of group consciousness such as in the domains of attitudinal reception (i.e., the perceptions that one's own ethnic group is the most deprived, that it receives fewer opportunities for adequate housing, education, or jobs, and that racial discrimination is an important problem in the community) and behavioral reception (i.e., the personal experiences of being discriminated against and of being verbally or physically abused because of one's ethnic background). Ethnicization can also be measured by indicators of structural integration (i.e., having crossracial friendship) and marital integration (i.e., not opposing interracial/ethnic marriage).

For Asians in Southern California, there are a few more possible indicators of panethnic or racial formation. These indicators are: (1) the frequency of hearing racial slurs about the panethnic group, (2) naming of at least one of the following—Michael Woo, March Fong Eu, Jay Kim, and Daniel Inouye—as a prominent group political leader, (3) knowing the length of pan-group immigration history, and (4) knowing of the unfair deprivation of one sub-ethnic group in the past (internment of the Japanese in World War II) and support for remedial actions (awarding reparations). Dummy variables were created for these eleven indicators except those measuring the degrees of concern with racial discrimination in community, personal experience of discrimination, and the hearing of racial slurs against Asians. These ordinal measures are scored from 1 to 4 with the highest score assigned to the strongest degree of concern or the most frequent experience of discrimination.

Similarly, the formation of ethnicity for Koreans in Los Angeles is conceived to consist of a number of adaptation stages, which do not necessarily occur in any chronological order. Group consciousness attributable to behavior reception is measured by one's personal experiences of discrimination and hate crimes; that associated with attitudinal reception is indicated by the perception that one's own group condition is worse off than other minorities and that racism is the primary barrier holding Koreans back. Marital integration for Koreans is assessed by one's degree of approving interethnic/racial marriage[10] and structural integration by the incidence of having non-Korean friends.

However, a number of items exclusively present in the 1992 survey of Koreans serve as additional indicators of the complex process of immigrant ethnicization. Besides crossracial friendship, possible measures of structural integration include a dummy variable indicating one's membership in a church organization as well as two ordinal measures—the conducting of business with Koreans and/or non-Koreans and the frequency of speaking with white persons in a week. Korean American acculturation can be estimated by the extent of using English and/or Korean language(s) and media in everyday life and the level of English proficiency. The strength of identifying with one's ethnic background can be gauged by the perceived importance of Koreatown and the preservation of Korean culture for future generations in Los Angeles as well as by one's residing in a Korean neighborhood and the expectation to return to Korea sometime in the future. In a range of scores (i.e., 1 to 4 or 1 to 5), higher scores are assigned to those responses indicating greater support of intermarriage and greater ability and likelihood to use English, to speak with white persons, to do business with non-Koreans, and to value Korean culture and Koreatown.

THE STRUCTURES OF PANETHNICITY ACROSS RACIAL/ETHNIC GROUPS

Previous studies have found that the concept of (pan)ethnicity or (pan)ethnic identity is far from monolithic. Although the precise configuration of the process is still under dispute, the few recent studies that empirically examine the concept tend to differentiate among acculturation, ethnic attachment, and group consciousness or the levels of perceived prejudice and discrimination (Keefe and Padilla 1987; Williams and Ortega 1990; Lien 1994). To find out if a multidimensional structure of panethnicity exists in the two data sets, several principal component factor analyses were run using an oblique rotation.[11] Results for the Southern California sample are reported in Tables 3-1 to 3-3. To avoid confusion with the somewhat different composition of group identity for a specific ethnic group, results for the Korean sample are reported in chapter 5.

For both citizens and all respondents in the Southern California sample (Table 3-1), the concept of panethnicity has three dimensions: personal experience of racial discrimination, concern over a troubled group status, and acculturation through interracial friendship or marriage. For the Asian subsample (Tables 3-2 and 3-3), four items specific to the group are added to the analysis: know group history, know group leaders, secure group interest, and hear racial slurs against Asians. The concept of Asian American panethnicity is found to consist of one additional dimension: group deprivation, which is part of the group concern factor for the four panethnic groups and is negatively related to other dimensions for Asians. Another part of the group concern factor present in the entire sample, the racial problem, is closely related to the personal experiences of discrimination among Asians.

There are also some differences between the results excluding and including noncitizens in terms of the order or the composition of items within certain factors. For instance, while the experience of discrimination loads with the personal factor for Asian citizens (Table 3-2), it has a closer

Table 3-1

Principal Components of Panethnicity Among Citizens and All Respondents in
the Southern California Survey

(A) Among Citizens

| | Oblique Rotated Components[a] (N=970) | | | |
	I	II	III	Communality[b]
Personal Discrimination				
Victim of Hate Crime	.772			.637
Being Discriminated	.751	.317		.600
Concern over Group Status				
Perceive Group Condition Bad		.710		.574
Racial Discrimination a Problem	.376	.621		.462
Own Group Most Deprived	.385	.518	-.363	.505
Acculturation/Racial Integration				
Crossracial Friendship			.775	.642
Interracial Marriage			.607	.440
Eigenvalue	1.74	1.00	1.12	
Variance (%)	24.90	14.30	16.00	

B) Among All Respondents

| | Oblique Rotated Components[a] (N=1103) | | | |
	I	II	III	Communality[b]
Personal Discrimination				
Victim of Hate Crime	-.821			.683
Being Discriminated	-.700	.387		.586
Concern over Group Status				
Own Group Most Deprived		.657		.525
Racial Discrimination a Problem		.640		.475
Perceive Group Condition Bad	-.322	.580		.415
Acculturation				
Crossracial Friendship			.740	.644
Interracial Marriage			.688	.540
Eigenvalue [c]	1.01	1.70	1.16	
Variance (%)	14.50	24.20	16.60	

Note: [a] Only loading scores greater than .30 or smaller than -.30 are reported.
[b] A communality in factor analysis shows how much variance of an observed variable is
accounted for by the common factor. It is calculated by summing the squared factor
loadings of a variable. [c] An eigenvalue indicates how much of the variation in the original
group of variables is accounted for by a particular factor.

Table 3-2

Principal Components of Panethnicity Among Asian American Citizens in the Southern California Survey

	I	II	III	IV	Communality[b]
		Oblique Rotated Components[a] (N=131)			
Personal Discrimination					
Victim of Hate Crime	.651				.445
Being Discriminated	.618		-.354		.482
Hear Racial Slurs	.607				.503
Racial Discrim. a Problem	.599	.448			.550
Concern over Group Status					
Know Group Leaders		.643			.501
Perceive Group Condition Bad		.617			.541
Secure Group Interest		.612			.397
Group Deprivation					
Own Group Most Deprived			-.782		.645
Know Group History			-.691		.577
Acculturation					
Interracial Marriage				.768	.623
Crossracial Friendship		.333		.742	.647
Eigenvalue	2.06	1.47	1.26	1.11	
Variance (%)	18.80	13.30	11.50	10.10	

Note: (see Table 3-1)

Table 3-3

Principal Components of Panethnicity Among All Asian Respondents in the Southern California Survey

| | Oblique Rotated Components[a] (N=180) | | | | |
	I	II	III	IV	Communality[b]
Personal Discrimination					
Victim of Hate Crime	.721				.525
Hear Racial Slurs	.707				.614
Racial Discrim. a Problem	.576		-.427		.544
Concern over Group Status					
Know Group Leaders		.666			.462
Crossracial Friendship		.632			.518
Secure Group Interest		.595	-.357		.470
Perceive Group Condition Bad		.518		-.388	.434
Group Deprivation					
Know Group History			-.721		.581
Own Group Most Deprived			-.681		.574
Being Discriminated	.478		-.482		.460
Acculturation					
Interracial Marriage				.824	.710
Eigenvalue	2.05	1.58	1.16	1.09	
Variance (%)	18.60	14.40	10.60	9.90	

Note: (see Table 3-1)

relationship to the group deprivation factor for all Asian respondents (Table 3-3). Similarly, Asian citizens' having close friends of other races is an indicator of acculturation, but it loads with the concern over group status when noncitizens are included. In parts A and B of Table 3-1, the sign of the personal discrimination factor is reversed. This indicates that in contrast to the case with citizens, what accounts for the experience of discrimination for all respondents is opposite to the underlying reasons shaping acculturation and group concern. Because the reliability coefficient testing additivity of items in each dimension of panethnicity is no higher than .55, only those variables having the highest factor score for each dimension were entered in the regression analyses for the Southern California sample.[12]

SUMMARY

This chapter opens with a brief review of the general approaches to studying Asian American political participation which often fall into the descriptive or historical category. This is followed by the justifications for the need of a survey approach. The two datasets used in this micro-level study are introduced, along with the operational definitions of key concepts. The structure of political participation and panethnicity for respondents in the Southern California sample is examined using several principal component analyses. In the following chapter, indicators of primordial and constructed panethnicity join socioeconomic, demographic, and legal factors to explain the extent and incidence of Asian American political participation within the panethnic group and as compared to other groups in this microcosm of Southern California.

NOTES

1. Major social and behavioral science research funding resources such as the National Science Foundation often preclude Asians who are not Pacific Islanders from seeking minority grant support. In the political science discipline, a similar case of biases in editorial and grants-giving decision-making as documented by Hero (1992, 173-188) for Latinos may also be made concerning research on Asian Americans.

2. The sustained interest from the mainstream media since October 1996 on Asian American campaign contributions has been unprecedented. Only time can tell whether this signifies a new era of press coverage on Asian American politics.

3. The problem of small sample size in surveys is not limited to Asians. In the same exit poll, the percentage of Latino respondents is 2.3%—a percentage much lower than their 9.5% share of the nation's population in 1990.

4. This information is based on initial reports released by separate organizations to the news media. The final report on the exit poll results of the 1996 election is expected to be released by the National Asian Pacific American Legal Consortium later in 1997.

5. This may be a source of potential bias in results. The technique was used to increase the efficiency of sampling numerically-small and residentially-dispersed minorities. Readers should use caution in interpreting findings.

6. The use of "white" in the sample is short for "non-Hispanic white." This differs from census reports where, unless otherwise specified, "white" includes those with a Hispanic origin.

7. However, weighted results will only be reported for the Korean survey. Because the use of weights will significantly reduce the size of the Asian subsample in the Southern California survey, only unweighted data are used.

8. The respective factor score for each activity in the Southern California sample is as follows: Among all respondents, contact officials =.649, attend functions =.641, donate money =.638, political volunteer =.598, register =.725, and vote =.631. The Eigenvalue for participation other than voting is 2.37 with 39.5% of the variance explained and a standardized 4-item alpha of .70. Among Asians, contact officials =.767, attend functions =.727, donate money =.706, political volunteer =.631, register =.833, and vote =.824. The Eigenvalue for participation other than voting is 2.35 with 39.2% of the variance explained and a standardized 4-item alpha of .71.

9. The factor score for each of the indicators is as follows: citizenship intent =.616, naturalization =.819, and registration =.644. The Eigenvalue is 2.08 with 69.3 of the variance explained.

10. Another measure of marriage assimilation is whether a respondent ever married a person of another ethnicity or race. This is not applicable here because

in this Korean sample almost every married respondent (96% among all) had a Korean spouse. Besides, lacking information on the place and time of marriage, it is unrealistic to estimate outmarriage for a new immigrant group if most of the marriages took place in the homeland.

11. Oblique rotation is a conservative test of dimensionality. Principal component results using varimax rotation, which assumes independence among variables, however, produce very similar structures.

12. The indicators of ethnicity used in each set of regression analyses and the dimension of ethnicity each represents are as follows. For citizen respondents in the entire sample, victim of hate crime (personal discrimination), perceive group condition bad (concern over group status), crossracial friendship (acculturation/ integration). For all respondents in the entire sample, interracial marriage replaces crossracial friendship on the acculturation dimension; the rest is the same as for citizens. For citizen respondents in the Asian subsample, victim of hate crime (personal discrimination), know group leaders (concern over group status), perceive own group most deprived (group deprivation), and interracial marriage (acculturation). For all respondents in the Asian subsample, knowledge of group history replaces perception of own group being most deprived on the group deprivation dimension; the rest is the same as for Asian citizens.

The Political Participation of
Asian Americans in a Multiethnic Setting:
Results of the Southern California
Survey

COMPARING ASIAN AMERICANS TO OTHER
RACIAL/ETHNIC GROUPS IN THE AGGREGATE

The extent of political participation recorded in the Southern California sample is reported in Section I of Table 4-1. In the aggregate, the frequency results generally support the impression that Asians (and Latinos) participate at a rate much lower than whites or blacks—except that the naturalization rate of foreign-born Asians (42%) is much higher than that for Latinos (23%). However, when citizenship is controlled, the participatory disparity is significantly reduced, though it does not disappear, for registration and voting. Among those registered, the Latino voting rate is as high as that for blacks and non-Hispanic whites; however, Asians still vote less. The rates of Asian participation in other activities (including campaign donations) are also low when compared to whites' (but higher than Latinos'), with citizenship status failing to account for the difference.

A description of the sociodemographic background of the respondents can be found in Section II of Table 4-1. Not surprisingly, Asians are overrepresented in higher education and income categories, exceeding even the levels for non-Hispanic whites. However, about one out of ten Asians—the highest percentage of the four panethnic groups—also reports

Table 4-1

Percentage Distributions of Political Participation and its Correlates
Across Four Groups in Southern California

I. POLITICAL PARTICIPATION

	Asian	Latino	Black	White
Citizenship				
Citizens	70%	67%	97%	97%
N=	221	199	144	646
Voter Registration				
Registered	47(68)*	43(64)	84	84
-among registered-				
—Democrats	39	59	83	41
—Republicans	38	24	5	44
—Other Party	7	2	4	4
—No Party	16	15	8	11
N=	150	124	137	610
Voting				
Voted in 1992	37(53)	37(55)	68(71)	71(74)
(among registered)	78	86	84	88
—Clinton (D)	46	58	84	39
—Bush (R)	44	28	6	39
—Perot	10	14	10	21
N=	100	82	110	492
Participation Other Than Voting				
Participated	24(27)	16(18)	27	40
—Contact official	11(11)	9(13)	10	24
—Contribute $	12(14)	5(6)	9	21
—Attend meeting	8(10)	5(5)	7	14
—Volunteer	9(10)	5(5)	15	14
N=	(varies)			

*Entries in parentheses refer to the percentages among citizens.

Table 4-1—continued

II. SOCIODEMOGRAPHIC BACKGROUND

	Asian	Latino	Black	White
Education				
0-7th grade	7(1)			
8th grade	5(2)	1	1	
9-11 grade	6(4)	11(10)	4	3
12th grade	10(8)	23(23)	20	16
Technical training	3(3)	11(14)	16	9
Some college	30(33)	28(35)	42	33
College degree	31(31)	9(9)	11	21
Some graduate work	8(9)	3(5)	1	4
Graduate degree	12(12)	3(2)	6	13
N=	218(153)	198(133)	142	646
Family Income				
Less than $10K	6(3)	7(4)	12	5
$10K-$19,999	10(7)	24(16)	23	11
$20K-$29,999	14(14)	20(19)	19	13
$30K-$39,999	17(17)	20(25)	14	20
$40K-$49,999	13(15)	11(13)	12	13
$50K-$59,999	9(10)	11(13)	11	11
$60K or more	31(34)	7(10)	8	27
N=	203(147)	186(126)	133	593
Employment				
Work full-time	45(50)	55(54)	50	42
Work part-time	8(9)	12(12)	7	8
Self-employed	8(8)	5(7)	8	13
Homemaker	5(3)	14(9)	4	8
Student	17(14)	4(4)	3	1
Look for work	9(7)	5(5)	6	4
Not look for work	1(1)	1(2)	1	1
Disabled	1(1)	2(2)	4	1
Retired	6(7)	4(6)	19	22
N=	220(154)	199(133)	144	646

*Entries in parentheses refer to the percentages among citizens.

Table 4-1—continued

	Asian	Latino	Black	White
Age				
18-21	18(15)	10(10)	4	3
22-24	10(10)	11(7)	3	5
25-39	39(35)	51(49)	43	31
40-44	12(14)	8(8)	8	10
45-64	14(17)	18(21)	24	27
65+	7(9)	3(5)	19	25
N=	218(153)	196(132)	144	638
Length of Stay in Southern California				
Fewer than 2 yrs	5(6)	2(0)	1	2
2-5 yrs	15(7)	11(5)	8	6
6-10 yrs	20(15)	12(8)	7	8
11-15 yrs	16(17)	11(8)	8	7
16-20 yrs	11(12)	9(5)	18	9
20 yrs+	14(20)	19(24)	33	40
Whole life	19(26)	37(51)	26	27
N=	220(154)	199(133)	144	646
Immigration Generation				
First generation	52(42)	35(23)	8	11
Second generation	34(38)	40(41)	6	15
Third or more gen.	14(20)	25(35)	86	74
N=	220(154)	198(133)	144	641
Gender				
Female	48(54)	48(49)	62	53
N=	220(154)	199(133)	144	646

III. SOCIO-PSYCHOLOGICAL FACTORS

A. Group Consciousness

*Entries in parentheses refer to the percentages among citizens.

Table 4-1—continued

	Asian	Latino	Black	White
Own Group Most Deprived				
Asian	**18(15)**	8(5)	3	8
Latino	37(40)	**63(54)**	56	33
Black	35(38)	42(46)	**78**	25
White	2(3)	6(6)	7	**16**
N=	221(154)	199(133)	144	646
Group Condition Bad (% of those who think conditions are bad or very bad)				
Asian	**11(10)**	16(19)	10	16
Latino	49(48)	**43(41)**	50	43
Black	45(47)	46(45)	**67**	47
White	4(4)	8(10)	8	**18**
N=	(various)			
Racial Discrimination a Problem				
Major	9(7)	12(9)	26	9
Moderate	25(27)	34(28)	25	28
Minor	43(41)	32(37)	27	37
No	24(25)	22(27)	22	26
Personal Experience of Discrimination				
Great deal	3(5)	5(3)	13	4
Fair	10(11)	9(9)	16	8
Some	51(51)	36(35)	47	31
None	37(33)	50(52)	25	58
N=	221(154)	196(130)	143	639
Ways Discriminated (among those being discriminated)				
Jobs	20(20)	27(21)	42	20
Education	8(6)	7(8)	8	6
Housing	3(3)	6(6)	19	2
Government	10(8)	5(5)	3	7
Business	18(22)	8(8)	29	8
Neighbor	7(7)	4(4)	2	3
Stranger	30(34)	14(14)	15	11
N=	(various)			

Table 4-1—continued

	Asian	Latino	Black	White
Victim of Hate Crime				
Victimized	18(17)	14(14)	18	12
N=	217(150)	198(132)	141	641
Hear Racial Slurs About Asians				
Very often	12(11)	13(14)	6	5
Fairly often	14(13)	21(19)	12	10
Fairly infrequent	26(28)	23(22)	26	28
Very infrequent	48(48)	44(46)	56	57
N=	216(151)	195(133)	139	643
Know of Asian American Political Leaders				
Name one+	38(42)	22(29)	24	26
Mike Woo	25(25)	21(26)	25	16
D. Inouye	9(13)	4(5)	2	11
Connie Chung	9(11)	9(7)	7	6
N=	221(154)	199(133)	144	646
Know of Asian American History				
100+ years	58(63)	43(52)	57	66
N=	202(142)	162(122)	122	587
Know of Internment of Japanese Americans				
Know	89(90)	85(86)	91	94
N=	187(136)	160(110)	118	609
Support Reparations				
Favor strongly	59(63)	41(39)	32	42
Favor somewhat	27(24)	29(28)	17	26
Oppose somewhat	6(4)	14(14)	14	13
Oppose strongly	8(9)	16(19)	36	19
N=	194(141)	176(119)	127	612

*Entries in parentheses refer to the percentages among citizens.

Table 4-1—continued

B. Acculturation/Integration

	Asian	Latino	Black	White
Crossracial Friendship				
Asian		31(38)	34	46
Latino	57(64)		50	67
Black	54(62)	52(60)		61
White	68(71)	35(36)	58	
Any Group	85(88)	72(78)	68	85
N=	(various)			
Interracial Marriage				
Approve strongly	14(14)	12(13)	16	12
Approve somewhat	7(7)	7(6)	4	8
Not care	70(69)	70(73)	75	59
Disapprove somewhat	6(6)	5(4)	2	12
Disapprove strongly	3(3)	6(5)	3	9
N=	207(147)	187(126)	140	611

Source: The Los Angeles Times Poll #318, August 7-10, 1993, released through the Roper Center for Public Opinion Research.
*Entries in parentheses refer to the percentages among citizens.

being unemployed at the time of the interview. Both the Asian and Latino groups are clearly younger than the black and white groups. About two-thirds of the respondents in the two recent immigrant groups are younger than 40; in contrast, those over 65 occupy a relatively small proportion in each of the two subsamples. In terms of the length of stay in the Southern California community, a higher percentage of Asians arrived within the last fifteen years than any other group, while over half of the respondents in the three non-Asian groups have lived in the area for at least twenty years. A similar trend is evident in the distribution of immigration generation across the groups. About half of all Asians were born outside the United States, whereas at least two-thirds of blacks and whites have U.S.-born parents. The distribution of Latinos across generations is more even, with slightly over one-third of the subsample falling into each of the first two generations.

As to those socio-psychological indicators of panethnicity, Asians, like their white counterparts, are quite positive about their experiences in Southern California. Few Asians think their own group suffers the most discrimination (18%) or have fewer opportunities for getting adequate housing, education, or jobs (11%). Most of them do not think racial discrimination is a serious problem in the community (67%); though about two-thirds of them have experienced at least some degree of personal discrimination, primarily from dealing with strangers (30%). Less than one-fifth of Asians (18%) report having been victimized because of one's ethnicity, but a higher percentage of Asians (26%) report hearing racial slurs about Asians in interpersonal communications.

The development of minority group identity can also be indicated by one's knowledge about group immigration history and prominent political leaders. About four out of ten Asians can name at least one prominent group political leader. Michael Woo is the most recognized personality; others include U.S. Senator Daniel Inouye, March Fong Eu, and U.S. Representative Jay Kim. About six out of ten Asians report knowing the correct length of Asian immigration (58%), but a greater percentage of whites know the length of Asian American immigration history (66%). One blatant example of the deprived Asian group status is the internment of Japanese Americans during World War II. About nine out of ten persons of Asian origin know of this historical event and almost an equal percentage of Asians favor awarding reparation payments to those who were interned.

Another factor influencing the development of a panethnic group identity in America is acculturation/adaptation. This is when members of a racial/ethnic group develop their sense of belongingness to the American community. Two of the stages in the adaptation of immigrant groups to American society are structural and marital integration. Based on these two accounts of survey results, Asians have a very high rate of social integration. The percentage of those persons reporting having a close friend of another race is as high as that of whites' (85%); and only one out of ten Asians opposes the idea of having someone in the family marrying a person of a different racial or ethnic background.

UNDERSTANDING ASIAN AMERICAN PARTICIPATION IN A COMPARATIVE PERSPECTIVE

One of the basic questions asked in this study is whether Asian American group identity matters for political participation. The logistic regression estimations of citizens' voting turnout and all respondents' participation in activities other than voting within the four-group sample are reported in Tables 4-2 and 4-3. As shown in column I of both tables, Latinos and Asians can be predicted to turn out or participate less than whites simply by their self-identified group identity. Although blacks voted at a rate equal to whites, they also tend to participate in other activities less than whites. A similar relationship between the group culture factor and the extent of other participation is observed in the multiple regression results in Table 4-4. Thus, when minority group culture is considered alone, Asian panethnicity, as well as Latino or even African American panethnicity, does matter in terms of (the lack of) political participation.

To account for the participatory disparity between the white majority and the racial/ethnic minorities, I first turn to socioeconomic factors. Results in column II of Tables 4-2 to 4-4 indicate that, although education and income variables relate strongly to the level of turnout as well as the incidence and extent of participation in other types of activities, they are

Table 4-2
Logistic Regression Estimations of Citizens' Registration and Voting
Participation in Southern California, 1993 (N=957)

Models	I	II	III	IV	Registration
(1) Group Culture					
Black	-.22	.10	.17	.17	.47
	(.22)	(.23)	(.24)	(.25)	(.30)
Latino	-.85***	-.54*	-.38	-.35	-.46
	(.21)	(.22)	(.23)	(.23)	(.25)
Asian	-1.02***	-1.33***	-1.12***	-1.10***	-.91**
	(.19)	(.21)	(.22)	(.22)	(.24)
(2) Socioeconomic Status					
Education		.36***	.41***	.40***	.42***
		(.06)	(.06)	(.06)	(.07)
Income		.15***	.18***	.17***	.11*
		(.04)	(.05)	(.05)	(.05)
Unemployed		-.43	-.14	-.15	-.02
		(.31)	(.32)	(.32)	(.35)
(3) Demographic					
Length			.20***	.20***	.22***
			(.05)	.05)	(.05)
Age			.024***	.027***	.038***
			(.005)	(.005)	(.006)
Male			-.24	-.24	-.10
			(.16)	(.16)	(.18)
(4) Socio-psychological					
Personal Discrimination				.13	.25
				(.23)	(.26)
Concern over Group Status				.28	-.08
				(.16)	(.18)
Acculturation/Integration				.30	.61*
				(.22)	(.24)
Constant	1.13***	-1.61***	-4.09***	-4.59***	-4.49***
	(.10)	(.33)	(.52)	(.57)	(.63)
Initial -2 Log Likelihood		1183 (I-IV)			978
At Convergence	1146	1057	1001	995	810
% Correct	69.17	72.41	75.65	74.92	81.30

Note: The dependent variable in models I-IV is scored 1 if the respondent reported voting for the president in 1992. Numerical entries are logistic coefficients except where noted. Standard errors are in parentheses.
* p<.05 ** p<.01 *** p<.001

Table 4-3

Logistic Regression Estimations of Participation Other Than
Voting in Southern California, 1993 (N=1094)

Models	I	II	III	IV	V
(1) Group Culture					
Black	-.42*	-.15	-.15	-.17	-.21
	(.21)	(.22)	(.22)	(.23)	(.23)
Latino	-1.28***	-.88***	-.79***	-.77**	-.63**
	(.22)	(.23)	(.24)	(.24)	(.24)
Asian	-.66***	-.81***	-.69***	-.69***	-.52*
	(.18)	(.19)	(.20)	(.20)	(.21)
(2) Socioeconomic Status					
Education		.26***	.27***	.26***	.23***
		(.05)	(.05)	(.05)	(.05)
Income		.15***	.16***	.17***	.15***
		(.04)	(.04)	(.04)	(.04)
Unemployed		.13	.22	.19	.16
		(.30)	(.31)	(.31)	(.32)
(3) Demographic					
Length			.05	.05	.03
			(.04)	(.04)	(.05)
Age			.007	.010*	.006
			(.004)	(.005)	(.005)
Male			-.15	-.16	-.14
			(.14)	(.14)	(.14)
(4) Socio-psychological					
Personal Discrimination				.59**	.58**
				(.19)	(.19)
Concern over Group Status				.26	.27
				(.15)	(.15)
Racial Integration/Acculturation				.24	.19
				(.20)	(.21)
(5) Legal					
Naturalization/Citizenship [a]					.30
or					(.29)
Registration					.82***
					(.19)
Constant	-.42***	-2.79***	-3.40***	-3.96***	-3.90***
	(.08)	(.32)	(.44)	(.49)	(.50)
Initial -2 Log Likelihood=1370					
At Convergence	1325	1254	1247	1233	1214
% Correct	68.10	70.02	70.29	71.30	71.66

Note: (see Table 4-2). The dependent variable is scored 1 if the respondent engages in any political activity other than voting and 0 otherwise.

[a] The partial coefficient for citizenship is taken from a separate model. Compared to other coefficients in the model using registration (column V), the significance of Asian ethnicity increases to p=.0018 and age has a borderline impact (p=.0523); the rest are no different in either model.

Table 4-4
Multiple Regression Estimations of Participation Other Than
Voting in Southern California, 1993 (N=1108)

Models	I	II	III	IV	V
(1) Group Culture					
Black	-.21**	-.10	-.09	-.13	-.14
	(.08)	(.07)	(.07)	(.08)	(.08)
Latino	-.38***	-.19**	-.15*	-.16*	-.14
	(.07)	(.07)	(.07)	(.07)	(.07)
Asian	-.25***	-.29***	-.25***	-.25***	-.23***
	(.06)	(.06)	(.06)	(.06)	(.07)
(2) Socioeconomic Status					
Education		.100***	.097***	.095***	.090***
		(.015)	(.015)	(.015)	(.015)
Income		.059***	.063***	.068***	.065***
		(.013)	(.013)	(.013)	(.013)
Unemployed		-.062	-.029	-.048	-.048
		(.099)	(.100)	(.099)	(.099)
(3) Demographic					
Length			-.004	-.006	-.013
			(.014)	(.014)	(.014)
Age			.045**	.051**	.045*
			(.017)	(.017)	(.018)
Male			-.031	-.041	-.038
			(.046)	(.046)	(.046)
(4) Socio-psychological					
Personal Discrimination				.303***	.301***
				(.064)	(.064)
Concern over Group Status				.040	.044
				(.057)	(.057)
Acculturation/Integration				.014	.004
				(.061)	(.061)
(5) Legal					
Naturalization/Citizenship [a]					.014
or					(.080)
Registration					.112*
					(.057)
Constant	.58***	-.30**	-.45***	-.54***	-.52***
	(.03)	(.10)	(.13)	(.14)	(.14)
Adj-R^2	.03	.11	.12	.13	.14
F	13.62***	24.37***	17.18***	15.11***	14.29***

Note: Numerical entries are regression coefficients except where noted. Standard errors are in parentheses. * $p<.05$ ** $p<.01$ *** $p<.001$

The dependent variable is scored by the summed value of participation in any of the activities other than voting and has a range between 0 and 4.

[a] The coefficient for citizenship is taken from a separate model where other coefficients are similar to those in column V, except that the Latino coefficient is also significant ($p=.04$).

not sufficient to account for the turnout or participation deficit between whites and Asians or Latinos. However, the reduced significance of the Latino group label in two of the three cases indicates that the SES model may be more useful for Latinos than for Asians. Yet, the disappearance of the significance of the black group label for other participation demonstrates that the SES model works best for the black group. In contrast, after controlling for SES factors, the Asian turnout and participation deficit is even larger than indicated by group label alone.

The addition of demographic factors does not seem to help much in accounting for the under-participation of Asians either. As shown in column III of Tables 4-2 to 4-4, the slope coefficients for Asian identity are smaller than in the socioeconomic models but not smaller than the group culture models and remain significant at p=.001 level. By comparison, the Latino citizens' disadvantages in length of stay and age, as well as education and income, help explain the differences between their turnout level and that of whites. None of the demographic factors are associated significantly with the incidence of Asian or Latino participation, but age seems to help account for the lesser degree of participation among Latinos.[1]

Past research indicates that the participation deficit of Asians cannot be explained away by sociodemographic and group consciousness variables. Results shown in column IV of Tables 4-2 to 4-4 appear to support this assessment. The addition of socio-psychological factors has little effect on the sizes of the slope coefficients associated with the Asian group label; they remain highly significant in indicating the lower levels of turnout or participation in other activities among Asians.[2] Although none of the socio-psychological factors has a significant relationship to voting turnout, controlling for personal experience of discrimination (being victimized) appears to help reduce the Latino deficit in the probability of participation in activities other than voting.

The last column in Tables 4-3 and 4-4 compares the effects of legal factors such as registration and citizenship status when differences in socioeconomic, demography, and socio-psychological factors are controlled. As hypothesized, being registered may be associated with a greater likelihood or higher level of participation in activities other than voting. It may also help account for the reduction of participation deficit between Asians and whites beyond the group culture variable. Being or becoming a U.S. citizen, however, may not be associated with an increased participation in activities other than voting. Although it would be interesting to estimate the effect of registration on citizens' voting turnout, there are concerns about the possible violation of the statistical assumption of independence. A separate run using registration as a dependent variable (shown in the last column of Table 4-2) indicates that the predictors of registration are similar to those of voting; but citizens who make more crossracial friends are also more likely to register. Among those who are registered, another logistic regression result (not shown) indicates that their likelihood of voting may relate negatively to the Asian label but positively to greater education, family income, and concern over group status.

In the end, these comparisons among panethnic groups highlight the degree of distinction of Asian American political participation. Despite controls over four different sets of factors that are often found to determine American political participation, Asians simply do not turn out or participate as much as the majority members of the American society, let alone participate more because of their higher overall socioeconomic achievement. What then influences the probability and extent of Asian political participation? Can we conclude from results comparing Asians to other racial/ethnic groups that SES and other factors do not have independent impacts on Asian turnout/participation?

SORTING OUT CORRELATES OF PARTICIPATION

Part of the answers to the questions raised above can be visualized by charting out the relationships between education/income and voting/participation across four groups (Figures 1 to 4). For Asians, the educational and income payoffs in terms of voting turnout are the lowest among the four groups. However, within each of the four groups, more education generally has the predicted effect of facilitating turnout. A similar but weaker case can be made for the income effect. Here for both Asians and blacks, turnout peaks at the family income level of $40K to $50K but resurges at the $60K or more level. In terms of the probability of participation in any of the four activities other than voting, education appears to have a very limited impact for Asians. Whereas those Asians

Figure 1

Voting of Racial/Ethnic Groups by Education

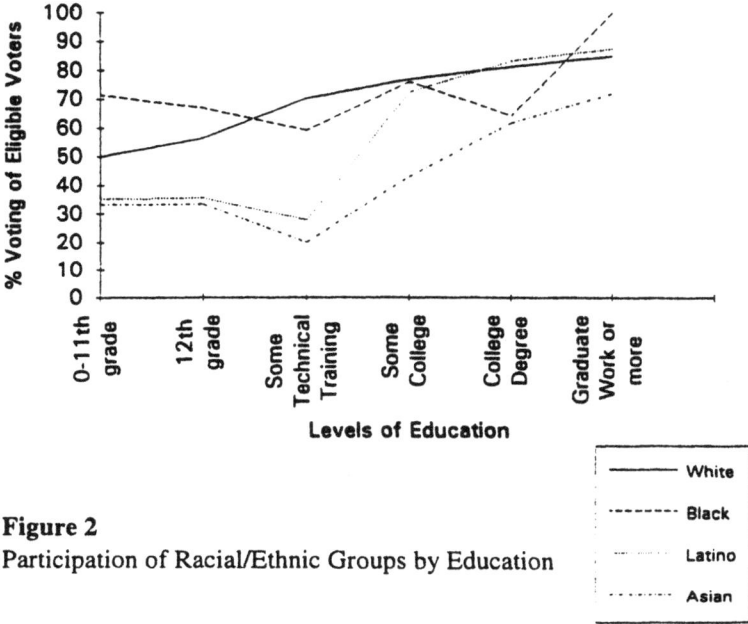

Figure 2

Participation of Racial/Ethnic Groups by Education

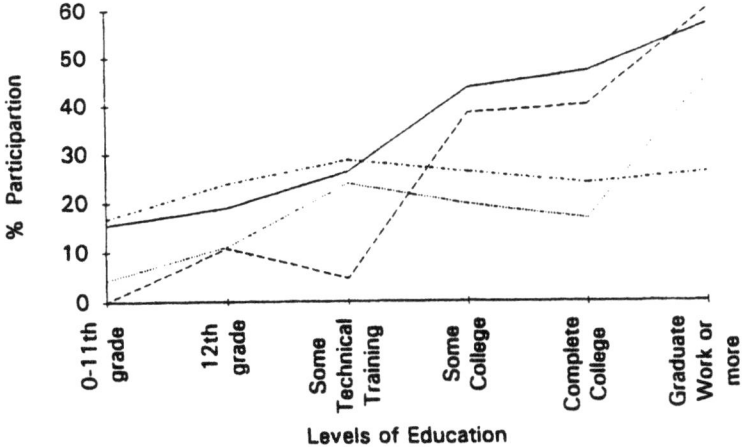

Figure 3

Voting of Racial/Ethnic Groups by Income

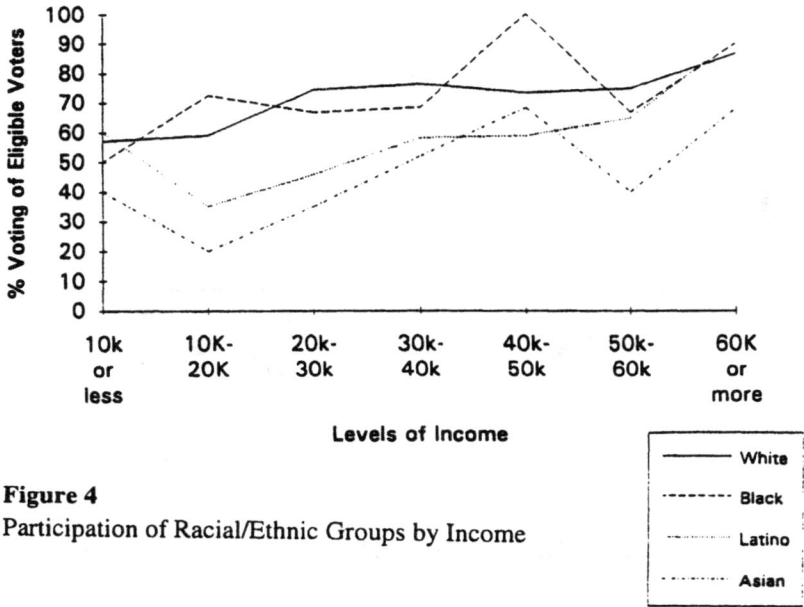

Figure 4

Participation of Racial/Ethnic Groups by Income

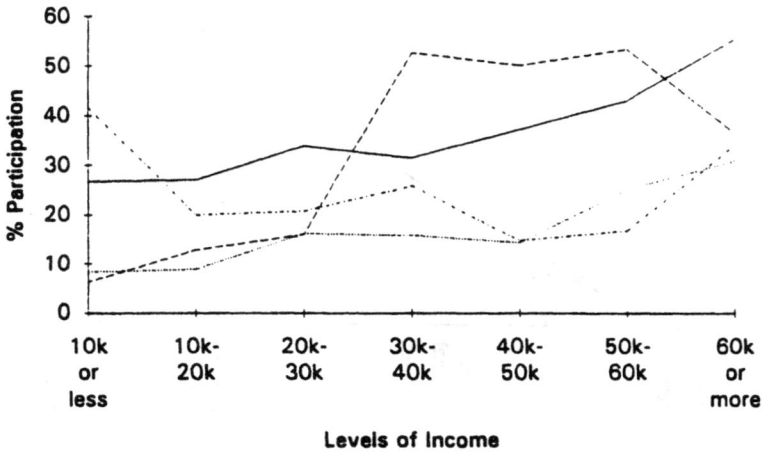

who did not attend college seem to participate at a rate higher than their counterparts in other racial/ethnic groups, those who achieve higher educational status do not participate more. Relatedly, the effect of income for Asians is almost concave, with those having the lowest and highest level of income participating more, but generally at a rate lower than other groups when income level reaches $40K. In sum, socioeconomic factors are less useful in explaining Asian turnout or participation. Compared to other groups, the payoffs for educational and income increments are either low or none. Although more education is correlated with higher turnout for Asian citizens, the effect of education on other types of participation and the overall effect of income diverge greatly from the patterns for whites.

This observation of the relative lack of usefulness of the socioeconomic factors in understanding turnout and participation within the Asian group is supported by analyses using logistic and multiple regressions. As shown in column II of Tables 4-5 to 4-7, when socioeconomic status is considered along with Asian ethnicity, education is the only significant determinant, but only for turnout among citizens. However, when demographic and socio-psychological factors are included, column IV of Table 4-5 indicates that income may replace the role of education in shaping turnout.

The efficacy of the demographic factors in explaining participation by Asians can be clarified by first comparing the effects of age and length of stay on voting and participation other than voting across the four groups. For Asian citizens, the impact of age is inconsistent (Figure 5). Whereas the turnout rate for those age 22 to 24 turnout is higher than that of their white counterparts, those over 40 years of age do not have a higher turnout rate than those in their early 20s. This is unlike the behavior of other groups. As for all Asian respondents in the survey, their probability of participation other than voting does not seem to change much as they age, except that those age 45 to 64 seem to be more active than others. Nevertheless, the Asian level of activism at all ages is consistently lower than that for whites (Figure 6). Among citizens, a longer length of stay in Southern California appears to have a stronger relationship to higher turnout for the three minority groups than it does for whites, but the slope for Asians is not as sharp as that for blacks or Latinos (Figure 7). Among all groups of respondents, participation fluctuates over one's years of stay

Table 4-5

Logistic Regression Estimations of Asian American Citizens' Registration and Voting Participation in Southern California, 1993 (N=131)

Models	I	II	III	IV	Registration
(1) Group Culture					
Japanese	-.01	.18	-.36	-.79	-.46
	(.49)	(.52)	(.63)	(.73)	(.78)
Korean	-.54	-.32	.04	-.63	-.84
	(.67)	(.72)	(.78)	(.89)	(.90)
Vietnamese	-1.08	-.91	-.61	-.59	.07
	(.58)	(.62)	(.68)	(.77)	(.75)
Filipino	-.32	-.15	-.14	.35	.29
	(.51)	(.55)	(.57)	(.65)	(.67)
(2) Socioeconomic Status					
Education		.37*	.37*	.29	.08
		(.16)	(.17)	(.19)	(.19)
Income		.14	.14	.34*	.35*
		(.12)	(.12)	(.15)	(.16)
Unemployed		.75	.99	1.02	.36
		(.74)	(.76)	(.81)	(.79)
(3) Demographic					
Length			.18	.10	.09
			(.13)	(.14)	(.14)
Age			.015	.040*	.058**
			(.014)	(.018)	(.020)
Immigration Generation			.24	.31	.07
			(.30)	(.34)	(.35)
Male			.42	.50	.02
			(.42)	(.48)	(.50)
(4) Socio-psychological					
Personal Discrimination				1.29	1.22
				(.75)	(.78)
Concern over Group Status				1.10*	.89
				(.50)	(.51)
Group Deprivation				1.68*	2.43*
				(.83)	(1.01)
Acculturation/Integration				2.13**	1.97**
				(.79)	(.69)
Constant	.53	-2.72*	-4.71**	-8.53***	-6.45**
	(.34)	(1.06)	(1.48)	(2.03)	(1.88)
Initial -2 Log Likelihood			179(I-IV)		163
At Convergence	175	162	157	134	149
% Correct	60.31	66.41	66.41	75.57	75.57

Note: The dependent variable in models I-IV is scored 1 if the respondent reported voting for the president in 1992. Numerical entries are logistic coefficients except where noted. Standard errors are in parentheses. * p<.05 ** p<.01 *** p<.001

Table 4-6

Logistic Regression Estimations of Asian American Participation Other Than Voting in Southern California, 1993 (N=173)

Models	I	II	III	IV	V
(1) Group Culture					
Japanese	.73	.78	.77	.86	.90
	(.48)	(.49)	(.53)	(.56)	(.57)
Korean	1.34*	1.48*	1.54*	1.32*	1.36*
	(.60)	(.62)	(.64)	(.66)	(.68)
Vietnamese	.31	.36	.44	.44	.33
	(.59)	(.61)	(.62)	(.66)	(.65)
Filipino	-.12	-.02	-.06	.10	.01
	(.57)	(.58)	(.59)	(.62)	(.63)
(2) Socioeconomic Status					
Education		.04	.05	.06	.04
		(.13)	(.14)	(.15)	(.15)
Income		.07	.06	.08	.03
		(.11)	(.11)	(.12)	(.12)
Unemployed		.72	.79	.84	.80
		(.57)	(.59)	(.61)	(.61)
3) Demographic					
Length			.04	.01	-.05
			(.11)	(.12)	(.12)
Age			.005	.007	.000
			(.014)	(.014)	(.015)
Immigration Generation			-.01	-.07	-.12
			(.27)	(.29)	(.29)
Male			-.21	-.27	-.16
			(.38)	(.40)	(.41)
(4) Socio-psychological					
Personal Discrimination				1.04*	.97*
				(.48)	(.49)
Concern over Group Status				-.02	-.14
				(.41)	(.42)
Group Deprivation				.37	.23
				(.41)	(.42)
Integration/Acculturation				.95	.73
				(.70)	(.71)
(5) Legal					
Naturalization/Citizenship [a]					.64
or					(.57)
Registration					.90
					(.48)
Constant	-1.46***	-2.21*	-2.45*	-3.68**	-2.96*
	(.35)	(.93)	(1.17)	(1.38)	(1.43)
Initial -2 Log Likelihood (for all)		197			
At Convergence	189	186	186	178	174
% Correct	74.57	74.57	74.57	77.46	78.61

Note: (see Table 4-5) The dependent variable is scored 1 if the respondent engages in any political activity other than voting and 0 otherwise.

[a] The partial coefficient for citizenship is taken from a separate model which uses citizenship as a legal factor. The coefficients for all other variables are nearly equal to the legal model using registration.

The Political Participation of Asian Americans

Table 4-7

Multiple Regression Estimations of Asian American Participation Other Than Voting in Southern California, 1993 (N=175)

Models	I	II	III	IV	V
(1) Group Culture					
Japanese	.07	.09	.01	.049	.050
	(.13)	(.14)	(.15)	(.147)	(.147)
Korean	.36*	.40*	.42*	.324	.327
	(.18)	(.19)	(.19)	(.186)	(.186)
Vietnamese	.16	.16	.22	.241	.217
	(.16)	(.16)	(.17)	(.169)	(.170)
Filipino	-.05	-.04	-.08	.006	-.005
	(.14)	(.15)	(.15)	(.150)	(.150)
(2) Socioeconomic Status					
Education		.016	.011	.005	.003
		(.038)	(.040)	(.040)	(.040)
Income		.006	.000	.005	.000
		(.029)	(.030)	(.030)	(.030)
Unemployed		.172	.210	.184	.179
		(.172)	(.174)	(.171)	(.171)
(3) Demographic					
Length			.013	.006	-.001
			(.030)	(.029)	(.030)
Age			.049	.055	.047
			(.039)	(.038)	(.039)
Immigration Generation			.084	.066	.061
			(.076)	(.075)	(.075)
Male			-.084	-.112	-.101
			(.107)	(.106)	(.107)
(4) Socio-psychological					
Personal Discrimination				.459**	.449**
				(.141)	(.142)
Concern over Group Status				.054	.040
				(.108)	(.109)
Group deprivation				.132	.117
				(.105)	(.107)
Acculturation				.130	.098
				(.146)	(.150)
(5) Legal					
Naturalization/Citizenship [a]					-.040
or					(.138)
Registration					.111
					(.117)
Constant	.26**	.10	-.14	-.359	-.269
	(.09)	(.26)	(.32)	(.332)	(.345)
Adj-R^2	.010	.000	.004	.062	.061
F	1.45	1.00	1.06	1.77*	1.71*

Note: (see Table 4-5) Numerical entries are regression coefficients except where noted. The dependen variable is scored by the summed value of participation in any of the activities other than voting anc has a range between 0 and 4.

[a] The coefficient for citizenship is taken from a separate model using citizenship as a legal factor. The rest of the coefficients in this model differ little from those in the model using registration.

Figure 5
Voting of Racial/Ethnic Groups by Age

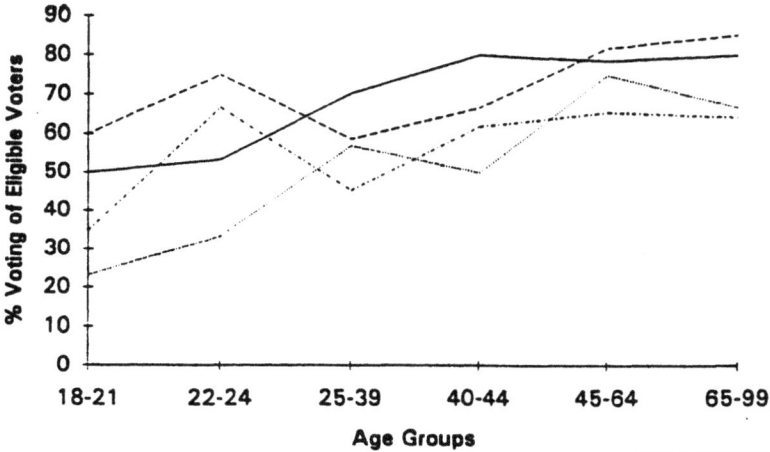

Figure 6
Participation of Racial/Ethnic Groups by Age

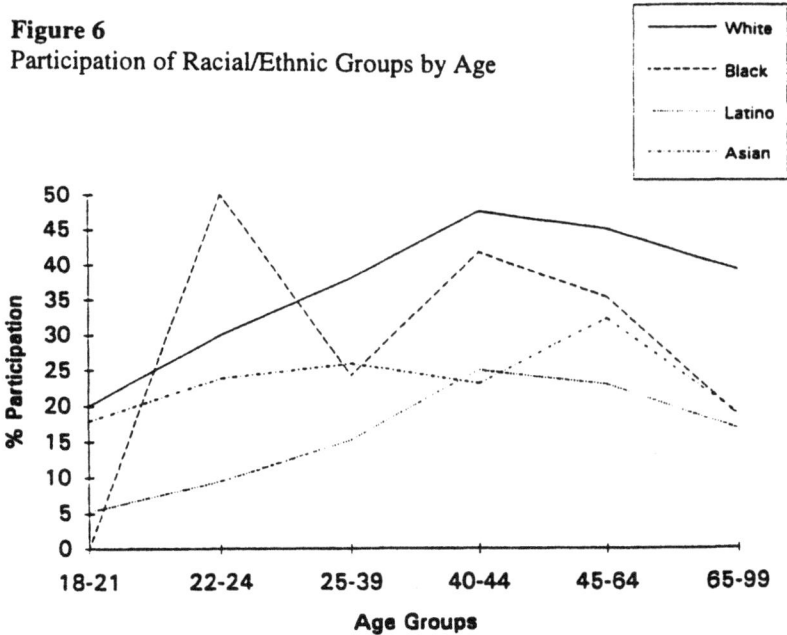

Figure 7
Voting of Racial/Ethnic Groups by Length of Stay

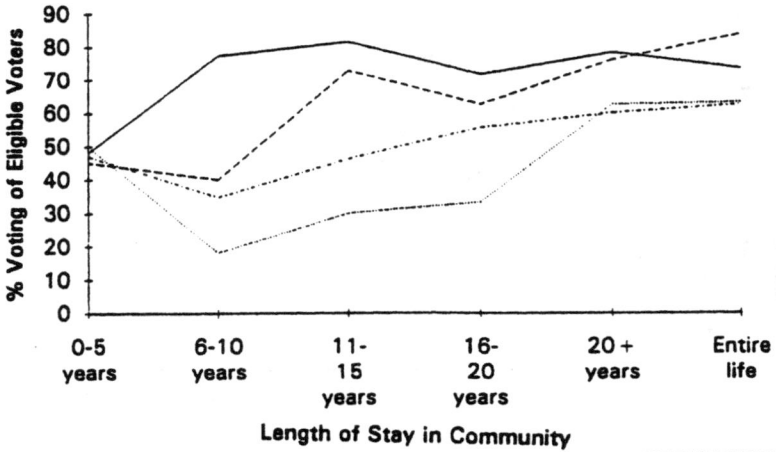

Figure 8
Participation of Racial/Ethnic Groups by Length of Stay

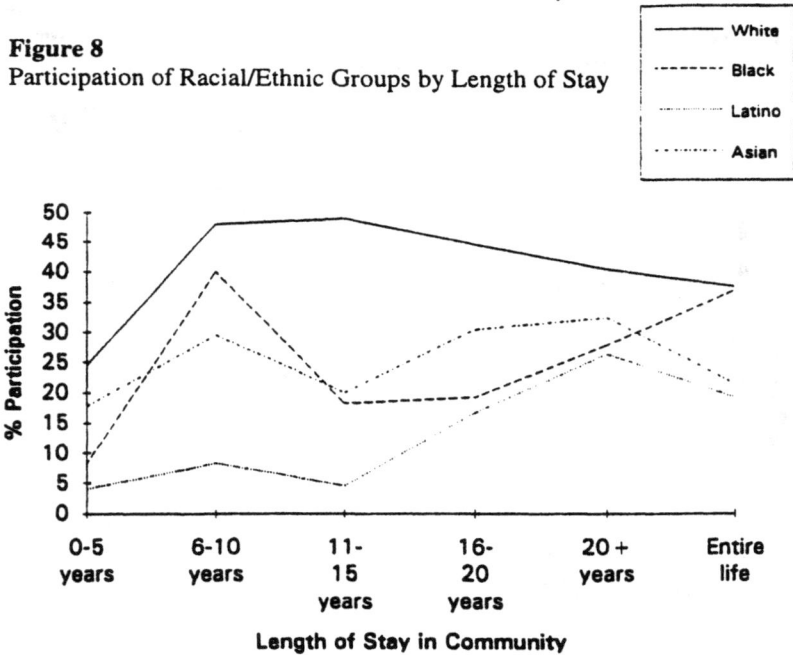

and Asians share a similar pattern, but at a higher level of participation, with Latinos (Figure 8).

It can be concluded from the discussion on the impact of demographic factors that the patterns for Asians are dissimilar to those for whites. This may explain the lack of efficacy demographic variables have in terms of accounting for the Asian participation deficit. When age, length of stay, immigration generation, and gender are controlled along with socioeconomic and group culture factors, results from column III of the three Asian tables indicate that demographic factors are also not useful in predicting the participation pattern among Asians.[3]

Yet, age does seem to have a relationship to turnout when socio-psychological factors are taken into account. Among Asian citizens, those who are older, more knowledgeable of their group political leaders, and believe that Asians are the racial/ethnic group that suffers the most discrimination in the society, and do not oppose a family member marrying someone of another race, are more likely to turn out to vote. The positive role of socio-psychological factors in explaining turnout patterns among Asian citizens differs sharply from its negligible role in models where citizens of all four groups are included. The addition of socio-psychological factors also helps to explain the probability and extent of participation among Asians.

Nevertheless, of the socio-psychological factors used to predict participation other than voting, what matters for all Asians is the personal experience of being victimized because of one's race. This is the same socio-psychological factor that is associated with greater participation other than voting for the four-group sample, but it is also the only socio-psychological factor that has no relationship to citizens' voting. Among all Asians, the indicator of personal discrimination helps account for the higher level of participation of Koreans as compared to that of the Chinese. It does not remove the difference in the likelihood of participation between the two Asian ethnic groups, although its addition reduces the size of the Korean slope coefficient.

The relative efficacy of the legal factors within the Asian sample is reported in the last columns of Tables 4-6 and 4-7. Unlike findings for the four-group sample, neither citizenship nor registration has any relationship to participation in activities other than voting, when four additional sets of factors are controlled. The lack of significance of the legal factors may be that the differences between citizens and noncitizens or registrants and non-registrants are already controlled by other variables in the models. The absence of an association between citizenship status and participation may also be attributed in part to the dominant concern among recent Asian immigrants about family reunification rather than politics in their quest for citizenship (Portes and Rumbaut 1990). A logistic regression analysis using the incidence of U.S. citizenship as the dependent variable (not shown) indicates that within the Asian subsample, citizenship is more likely among those who are from Vietnam, male, older, have a higher level of family income, have more years of stay in Southern California, have a longer family history in the United States, and know about the length of Asian immigration in the U.S. history. Among Asian citizens, registration is more likely if one is older, has a higher level of family income, knows about Asian immigration history, and is not opposed to interracial marriage (last column of Table 4-5). These are the same factors that explain Asian turnout.

The degree of diversity within Asian America is a topic that is receiving increasing attention. How much can one predict the political participation of Asians by their specific ethnic group origin? Results from Table 4-5 suggest that divergent Asian ethnicity does not necessarily relate to different levels of voting turnout among citizens in the Southern California sample. This is true whether other variables are controlled or not. Knowing a respondent's Asian ethnicity can increase our ability to predict voting turnout by 7%. However, Asian citizens with Japanese, Korean, Vietnamese, or Filipino ancestry do not turn out significantly less than their Chinese counterparts.

Being Korean, though, makes one more likely to participate in other political activities in comparison to the Chinese. Being Korean also indicates higher levels of participation in other activities, but the significance of the Korean factor disappears when the personal experience of being a hate crime victim is taken into account. This appears to be a reasonable finding considering that the survey was taken after the traumatic Rodney King Riots of 1992. Besides, as explained by Light and Bonacich (1988), self-employed Korean immigrants in Los Angeles may be more heavily endowed with civic, social, political, and religious organizations within the ethnic community than non-Koreans. An exploration of the similarity and uniqueness of the Korean American experience as compared to the pan-Asian American experience is the topic of the next chapter.

SUMMARY

The preceding discussion in this chapter reveals a clear pattern—pan-Asian ethnicity does matter for political participation. Being an Asian significantly depresses one's likelihood of voting and participation in other political activities as compared to a white of non-Hispanic origin; and socioeconomic, demographic, socio-psychological, and legal factors have limited effect on explaining this pattern of relationship. However, this does not necessarily mean that these factors are not useful in understanding Asian turnout or participation. Among Asians of different ethnic origins, factors regarding a citizen's income, age, and attitudes toward group identity may be associated with his/her likelihood to vote; and a respondent's probability and extent of participating in other activities may correlate with one's experience of discrimination. Among the five models of participation, the socio-psychological model appears to be the most useful for understanding Asian turnout. This set of factors also seems to best explain the ethnic cultural differences in the extent of participation in activities other than voting. Whether similar patterns of relationship between socioeconomic, demographic, and socio-psychological factors and political participation can be observed within a specific Asian ethnic group—the Koreans in Los Angeles—is the focus of the next chapter.

NOTES

1. Age groups rather than raw age is used in multiple regressions so as to distinguish the possible impact due to the increments in age. Other means of measuring age-related impacts such as age-square and older (65 and over) to pick up the decline in participation in tail end are found to be insignificant in predicting participation. In models where age groups is a significant variable, the addition of an age-square variable can knock off the significance of age.

2. I also tested the effects of all the socio-psychological variables appearing in Table 4-1. The attempts failed as well to reduce the significance of the Asian group label in either voting or other participation.

3. A similar procedure was used to test the effect of time-related variables for Asians. In addition, the effects of age, immigration generation, and length of stay were tested respectively and found to be insignificant.

CHAPTER 5

Another Look at Asian American Ethnicity
Integration of Korean Immigrants in Los Angeles, 1992

By far, the majority of the discussion on the construction of ethnicity has been at the panethnic group level. Although we have gained some knowledge about the relationship between ethnicity and political participation at this level, it is unclear whether similar patterns would emerge if the concept of ethnicity is cast at the sub-Asian group level. In this chapter, one Asian ethnic group, Korean Americans, is examined to shed some light on this question.

KOREANS IN LOS ANGELES

Although the presence of Koreans in Los Angeles can be dated as far back as 1904, the Korean community did not begin to grow until after the passage of the 1965 Immigration Act. When the U.S. Bureau of the Census first counted Koreans as a distinct ethnic group in 1970, less than 9,000 were enumerated in Los Angeles County.[1] By the 1990 census, the Korean population in the County was 16 times larger. This remarkable rate of population expansion within a 20-year period resulted mainly from the convergence of U.S. immigration policy; homeland government emigration policy; political, social, and economic developments on both sides of the Pacific Ocean; the stationing of U.S. military personnel and the penetration of American enterprise in South Korea; and the revolutions in transportation and communication technologies (Kim 1981; Light and Bonacich 1988; Reimers 1992; Ong, Bonacich, and Cheng 1994). It can also be attributed to the high birthrate stemming from the favorable age-sex ratio of the immigrants (Yu 1982). However, among the over 145,000 Koreans enumerated in the 1990 census for Los Angeles County, only 17% (or 2% of those aged 24-64) were born in the United States and six of out of ten had not entered the United States until 1980 or later (Ong and Azores 1994). Given the high saliency of immigration in their background, the adaptation of Korean Americans to U.S. society and system is of ultimate concern to the studying of this ethnic group.

The Korean presence in Los Angeles is most visible in Koreatown, a residential and commercial area of about 25 square miles located west of downtown. About 3,000 Korean-owned businesses of all kinds with Korean-language signs are located here amidst numerous community and cultural organizations (Daniels 1990; Min 1995). In addition to the attractions of existing business and socio-cultural institutions in Koreatown, the formation of the largest Korean settlement in North America can be explained by some of the inviting features of the metropolitan area such as the abundance of public and private educational institutions, relatively low residential density in the central city, a convenient freeway system, and a mild climate (Kim and Wong 1977).

The emergence of the Korean community in Los Angeles is closely related to the high propensity of the members of the community to engage in small businesses (Lee 1992). Many immigrants, mostly college-educated and of middle-class background, are forced to start small retail stores (e.g., liquor stores, grocery marts, clothing shops, gas stations, etc.) in low-income black and Latino neighborhoods, largely because of discrimination in the labor market and their limited capital and English proficiency (Light and Bonacich 1988). They soon find themselves functioning as a "middleman minority"—simultaneously exploiting and being exploited in the economy of impoverished areas like South Central Los Angeles. However, the perception of Korean merchants taking money out of the poverty-stricken community deepens the sense of disillusionment of many area residents, who feel abandoned and betrayed by the established economic and political order. This perception contributed greatly to the targeting of Korean (and other Asian) businesses in the Los Angeles Riots of 1992 (Chang 1994; Freer 1994).

Whereas many have studied the sources and impact of the Riots and the status of cultural and economic integration of Korean immigrants, very little attention is paid to the political aspect of the adaptation process (exceptions include Cha 1977; Lee 1980; Jo 1982). To what extent have Korean immigrants as individuals been able to integrate into the mainstream political system? And what may account for the phenomenon?

This chapter uses a large-scale survey of Koreans in Los Angeles that was conducted on the eve of the Riots to study the scope and source of Korean immigrant political integration.

PRELIMINARY OBSERVATIONS FROM SUMMARY STATISTICS

As described in Chapter 3, the data for the *Los Angeles Times* Poll were collected by telephone interviewing a random sample of 750 adult Korean American residents, mostly in the Korean language, of Los Angeles County, California. Compared to the 1990 census of Koreans in the county, the respondents are overrepresented in being foreign-born and having higher education levels, about equally represented in having families with higher income, and underrepresented in citizenship status and voter registration. A detailed description of socioeconomic background and socio-psychological factors impacting levels of political participation appears in Table 5-1.

Within the entire sample, only about one-third (36%) has gone through the naturalization process and become U.S. citizens, although two-fifths of the noncitizens expect to become citizens in the near future. Of the 265 citizens, only about one-half are registered to vote. These rates are far lower than those reported in Table 4-1 (70% citizenship and 68% registration) for Asians as a whole. The 1992 survey does not include turnout data for the previous presidential election (1988). However, if the results reported in the preceding chapter for Asians in Southern California are an indication, correlates of Korean American voting turnout should not be much different from those for voting registration.

As noted, this sample, like the Asian sample from six counties, contains a very high percentage of college-educated respondents. Higher educational achievement, however, has not been found to increase the likelihood of participation for Asians. Part of the reason may be that these respondents in large part did not attend schools in the United States. Seven out of ten Koreans report having been educated only in Korea. At the bivariate level, the percentage of those having received education in Korea decreases as one becomes more engaged with the U.S. political system. However, higher education does appear to be associated with greater political involvement for the Korean sample. Similar correlations can also be observed with having a higher income, greater length of stay, being employed, and being male, but not with being older.

Table 5-1
Percentage Distributions of Political Participation and its Correlates among
Koreans in Los Angeles, 1992

I. POLITICAL PARTICIPATION

Citizenship (asked of all) N=750
Citizens   36%

Citizenship Intent (asked of noncitizens) N=485
Expect to   39%

Voter Registration (asked of citizens) N=265
Registered   51%
Democrats   44
Republicans   47
Other Party   0
No Party   9

II. SOCIODEMOGRAPHIC BACKGROUND

	Noncitizens Expected to Become Naturalized		Citizens Registered to Vote		All
	No%	Yes%	No%	Yes%	%
Education					
0-7th grade	4	3	1	0	2
8th grade	5	2	1	0	3
9-11 grade	4	8	2	1	4
12th grade	30	28	25	10	25
Tech. training	7	4	8	7	7
Some college	7	15	11	11	10
College degree	38	37	45	60	42
Some grad. work	5	4	3	7	5
Graduate degree	1	0	3	4	2
N=	289	186	127	124	726

Table 5-1—continued

	Noncitizens Expected to Become Naturalized		Citizens Registered to Vote		All
	No%	Yes%	No%	Yes%	%
Place of Education					
Korea	79	75	52	47	68
United States	2	3	15	36	11
Both	17	22	32	17	21
N=	295	186	130	134	745
Family Income					
Less than $10K	12	12	7	3	10
$10K-$19,999	18	18	12	4	14
$20K-$29,999	21	18	11	7	16
$30K-$39,999	16	11	15	20	15
$40K-$49,999	12	14	14	20	14
$50K-$59,999	6	16	20	14	12
$60K or more	15	12	23	32	19
N=	224	156	108	118	606
Employment					
Work full-time	38	40	52	52	44
Work part-time	10	8	10	11	10
Self-employed	9	8	13	13	10
Homemaker	23	21	12	10	18
Student	13	17	8	8	12
Look for work	2	1	1	1	
Not seek work	1	1	1	1	
Retired	4	4	3	5	4
N=	297	187	131	132	748
Age					
18-27	20	26	24	18	22
28-37	32	27	33	20	29
38-49	21	18	24	31	22
50-64	16	14	11	22	16
65+	11	16	8	9	11
N=	297	186	127	132	742

Table 5-1—continued

| | Noncitizens Expected to Become Naturalized | | Citizens Registered to Vote | | All |
	No%	Yes%	No%	Yes%	%
Length of Stay in the United States					
0-5 yrs	47	41	2	0	29
6-10 yrs	35	38	33	11	31
11-15 yrs	14	10	38	26	19
16-20 yrs	4	5	23	43	15
21+ yrs	0	5	4	19	5
N=	297	186	127	132	746
Nativity					
Korea-born	100	100	99	90	98
U.S.-born	0	0	0	2	0
N=	298	186	131	132	748
Gender					
Female	56	50	60	34	51
N=	298	187	131	134	749

III. SOCIO-PSYCHOLOGICAL FACTORS

A. Group Consciousness

Relative Group Condition					
Better	70	71	78	72	72
Worse	7	6	8	12	8
Same as	23	23	14	17	20
N=	280	180	124	128	712
Victim of Hate Crime					
Never	77	69	81	82	76
Race-related	18	28	16	16	20
Unrelated	6	3	3	2	4
N=	286	181	131	129	728

Table 5-1—continued

	Noncitizens Expected to Become Naturalized		Citizens Registered to Vote		All
	No%	Yes%	No%	Yes%	%
Personal Experience of Discrimination					
Not at all	56	61	54	40	54
Some, not much	33	27	38	48	35
A fair amount	9	9	8	8	9
A great deal	2	3	1	4	3
N=	278	176	126	127	707
Ways Discriminated					
None	47	50	44	46	49
Jobs	11	9	12	17	12
Education	10	8	6	2	7
Government	9	8	6	3	7
Business	10	8	7	11	8
Strangers	10	16	22	18	14
N=	274	183	121	133	678
Primary Barrier for Group					
Nothing	2	1	5	4	3
Racism	16	25	19	22	20
Language	54	48	45	46	49
Lack interest	8	6	9	7	7
Culture	16	17	21	17	17
No job train.	1	3	2	2	2
N=	280	182	130	129	721
B. Acculturation/Integration					
English Fluency					
Not at all	20	14	4	2	12
Not well	42	42	26	17	35
Just well	31	40	47	42	38
Very well	7	5	24	39	15
N=	296	185	130	134	745

Table 5-1—continued

	Noncitizens Expected to Become Naturalized		Citizens Registered to Vote		All
	No%	Yes%	No%	Yes%	%
Language Use					
Only English	1	6	11	3	
Mostly English	7	4	21	18	11
Equally	26	34	40	41	33
Mostly Korean	26	28	22	18	24
Only Korean	42	33	11	12	29
N=	298	186	131	132	747
Media Use					
Only English	1	3	11	13	5
Mostly English	15	14	22	32	19
Equally	31	34	31	38	33
Mostly Korean	24	23	24	5	20
Only Korean	29	27	11	12	22
N=	298	187	131	134	749
Business Contacts					
Only Non-Korean	11	7	16	18	12
Mostly Non-Korean	17	24	39	28	24
Equally	28	25	23	29	26
Mostly Korean	20	23	16	19	19
Only Korean	23	22	7	6	16
N=	282	179	131	132	724
Speaking with Whites					
None	26	20	9	8	18
1-5	23	30	26	20	25
5-10	11	22	11	8	13
10-25	21	12	15	11	16
25+	19	17	39	54	28
N=	289	185	130	132	736

Table 5-1—continued

	Noncitizens Expected to Become Naturalized		Citizens Registered to Vote		All
	No%	Yes%	No%	Yes%	%
Interracial Marriage					
Strongly disappr.	30	18	17	18	23
Somewhat disappr.	14	14	16	8	13
Don't care	7	4	3	10	6
Somewhat approve	38	47	30	35	38
Strongly approve	11	18	34	29	20
N=	286	177	126	130	719
Crossracial Friendship					
Yes	54	61	70	81	63
N=	298	187	131	134	744
Religious Affiliation					
Church Member	66	74	71	80	72
N=	297	187	128	134	745

C. Attachment to Ethnic Culture

Importance of Preserving Korean Culture					
Not very important	4	3	6	8	5
Fairly important	18	11	18	22	17
Very important	78	85	75	71	78
N=	288	186	130	134	737
Importance of Koreatown					
Not at all	5	0	5	6	4
Not as important	12	20	14	22	16
One of many	31	33	43	24	32
Most important	43	37	36	45	40
Live in it	9	10	3	4	7
N=	290	183	130	132	734

Table 5-1—continued

	Noncitizens Expected to Become Naturalized		Citizens Registered to Vote		All
	No%	Yes%	No%	Yes%	%
Racial Makeup of Neighborhood					
Mostly White	36	30	37	62	39
Mostly Black	2	3	5	2	3
Mostly Latino	6	22	4	6	9
Mostly Korean	19	12	10	3	13
Mostly Asian	7	5	11	8	7
Mixed	27	26	29	17	25
N=	297	187	131	132	747
Expect to Return to Korea					
Yes	35	15	11	6	20
N=	276	174	119	128	697

Source: The Los Angeles Times Poll #267, February/March 1992, released through the Roper Center for Public Opinion Research.

Compared to the Asian respondents in Table 4-1, income and age for this sample of Koreans are more evenly distributed. The median family income of Koreans ($30K-40K) is lower than that of Asians in general ($40K-50K); and the average Korean respondent is about five years older (40.5) than the average Asian respondent in the other survey. A roughly equal percentage of respondents in both surveys report being employed, but the percentage of homemakers is higher and the percentage of the unemployed is lower in the Korean sample. As is expected for a foreign-born immigrant group, more Koreans are in the shorter length of stay categories (mean=10 years) and far fewer have lived for over 20 years in the U.S. community.

The interviews were completed just one month prior to the 1992 Rodney King Riots in South Central Los Angeles where the depth of the multiracial/ethnic tension shocked the entire nation. The timing of and the questions asked in this survey permit an estimation of the degree of tension as perceived by Korean Americans living in the region. Appendix E summarizes results of a selected group of items exploring interethnic relations between Korean Americans and other minorities. Responses to these survey items, though not pursued in later analyses, provide a general context for understanding the meanings of group consciousness and ethnicity which are part of the main interests of this study.

On the eve of the Riots, many Korean respondents are concerned about tensions in race relations, but they generally do not perceive a worsening situation. Many attribute responsibility to both Koreans and blacks, but more think that the news media exaggerate the amount of conflict. Indeed, three out of four respondents are satisfied with the current way of life and think that racial tensions lag behind economic recession and crime as the most important problems in the region. However, the respondents have fewer contacts with blacks and a much more negative view of blacks than of Latinos.

Among the possible indicators of group consciousness, the condition of Koreans is judged to be mostly better off than other minorities in Southern California, but three out of ten respondents feel that the relative group condition of Koreans is about as bad or even worse off than other minorities. Two out of ten respondents report having been verbally or physically abused because of their race. Of the 47% of respondents that have experienced at least some form of discrimination, the majority do not perceive the amount to be great. About one-third attribute the source of discrimination to strangers in a public place, with a smaller proportion reporting incidents in the workplace. Yet, racism and discrimination are serious enough to be considered by 20% of Koreans as the primary barrier to group success in Southern California.

A similar proportion of Asian respondents report having fallen victim to hate crimes or being discriminated against a fair amount to a great deal in the six-county survey reported in Table 4-1. The sources of discrimination also appear to order in a similar fashion in both surveys. Yet, although a higher percentage of Koreans express no experience of discrimination at all, three times more respondents in the Korean survey find their group condition to be no better than other minority groups. It seems that for this group of newcomers to U.S. racial politics, a linkage has not yet been established between discriminatory experience and feelings of group deprivation.

Perhaps consequentially, a clear pattern does not exist between group consciousness and involvement across levels of participation. Those who are not naturalized appear to be more likely to fall victim to race-related crimes and to perceive their own group's condition as bad as that of other minorities, but they are also more likely to report no experience of discrimination. Registered voters, though, are more likely to perceive an inferior group condition relative to other minority groups, report having more experience of discrimination, and are less likely to name racism as the primary barrier than those who expect to become citizens. Moreover, though the registered voters seem to experience more discrimination in the workplace and social situations involving strangers, they are less likely to experience discrimination in education and government areas than the less integrated. These observations caution one against making an unidimensional assumption of immigrant group consciousness and its relationship to political participation.

The story appears to run differently when possible indicators of acculturation and social integration that generally correlate with levels of participation are added. For instance, higher percentages of fluency in and usage of English are found among those who are naturalized and/or registered to vote. A similar pattern is found with indicators of crosscultural friendship, support of interracial marriage, church membership, and mainstream business or other contacts. Yet, a relatively large percentage of the respondents have low acculturation. Close to half of the sample say that they are not at all fluent or not fluent enough in English. More than four out of ten Koreans rely mostly or exclusively on their native tongue for communication with others and with the outside world. With the exception of the near absence of outmarriage, the general level of structural integration appears to be quite high, with 63% of respondents having friends of other races and 72% being a member of a religious congregation. Still, about two out of five respondents do not speak with a single mainstream white person in an average week; a slightly smaller percentage of respondents report conducting business and financial transactions exclusively with Koreans; and some 23% of Koreans staunchly oppose the idea of intermarriage.

Relatedly, a large majority of Koreans perceive the preservation of ethnic culture as highly important. An equal amount of the sample think Koreatown in Los Angeles is the most, or one of the most, important place(s) as a business, cultural, and social center. Beyond the issue of social desirability with value-laden items in a survey, this (and other) strong showing of attachment to ethnic culture is impressive—given that except for a small portion (13%) of the respondents, all others live within non-Korean neighborhoods.

Yet, for foreign-born immigrants, residing among their own ethnic group members can significantly limit exposure and access to the mainstream. The result may be a reinforcement of identification with the homeland culture and an isolation from the mainstream culture. Residing in Korean neighborhoods is, therefore, treated separately from structural integration. Attachment to the homeland ethnic culture, and perhaps isolation from the mainstream, can also be estimated with one's intent of returning to the home country. Within this sample of Koreans, one out of five respondents expects to end up in Korea in the years to come. The level of intent and the likelihood to reside in a Korean neighborhood are highest among the least integrated. On the other hand, there is no clear pattern of a relationship between political integration and the perceived importance of Korean culture and Koreatown.

THE STRUCTURE OF KOREAN IMMIGRANT ETHNICITY

A few authors have done extensive research on the construction of Korean American ethnicity (Hurh 1980; Hurh and Kim 1984a, 1984b; Kim and Hurh 1993). The main conclusion of these studies is that the adaptation processes of Korean immigrants to the United States do not fall into either the assimilation or pluralism paradigm. Rather, they follow an additive mode of adaptation where the attachment to ethnic lifestyles and social network is not affected by the length of stay, despite the progress in acculturation over time. This is consistent with the discussion in previous chapters about the multiple processes underlying the concept of Asian

American ethnicity. However, the present study examines a fuller set of factors and adopts a different approach than the previous research done by Hurh and others.

Results of the principal component analysis with oblique rotation are reported in Table 5-2. In general, the results confirm the hypothesis that Korean American ethnicity is a multilayered concept. Similar to findings for Asians in the Southern California sample, Korean American ethnicity consists of dimensions of acculturation, personal discrimination, and group deprivation. The availability of additional items in the dataset also allows the detection of three other dimensions: attachment to ethnic culture, detachment from mainstream culture, and church membership. However, our understanding of the structure of immigrant ethnicity can be enhanced when the composition of each of the dimensions and their interrelationship are carefully examined.

In earlier discussions, acculturation is hypothesized to be indicated by the level of proficiency in the mainstream language (English fluency) and the frequency of its application in daily use (language use, media use); possible indicators of structural integration, on the other hand, include crossethnic/racial friendship, church membership, business contacts and oral communication with members of the mainstream group. The principal component results show that, except for church membership, indicators for the two dimensions can be explained by the same underlying factor.

The distinctive role of church membership in the construction of ethnicity is an interesting finding. Although the survey does not distinguish between membership with an English-language or Korean-language church, past studies have found that most Koreans attend Korean churches and that Christian churches, especially Protestant churches, are dominant in organizing and leading community activities including nonreligious, secular ones (Kim 1981). The dual role performed by the churches as a bridging organization between their congregations and the larger society and as a guardian of ethnic culture and tradition may explain the separate and negative coefficient for church membership in the analysis.

The dimension of ethnic attachment has previously been conceived to consist of perceived importance of the ethnic enclave and the preservation of ethnic culture, as well as having coethnic neighbors and the intent of returning to one's homeland. However, only responses to the first two items load into the hypothesized dimension. A second dimension, detachment from mainstream culture, is composed of the other two items along with the opposition to intermarriage. This not only indicates that factors shaping one's attachment to ethnic culture are structurally different

Table 5-2
Principal Components of Ethnicity Among Koreans in
Los Angeles, 1992

	I	II	III	IV	V	VI	Communality[b]
	Oblique Rotated Components[a] (N=661)						

	I	II	III	IV	V	VI	Communality[b]
Acculturation							
English Use	.855						.747
Fluency	.823						.712
Media Use	.792						.647
Speak w/ Whites	.724						.563
Business Contact	.674						.488
Friendship	.666						.496
Attachment to Ethnic Culture							
Preserve Culture		.779					.651
Value Koreatown		.738					.599
Detachment from Mainstream Culture							
Expect to Return			.621			.337	.539
Korean Neighbors			.621				.556
Support Intermarriage			-.607				.522
Group Deprivation							
Racism Main Barrier					-.711		.548
Group Condition Worse	-.314			.360	-.438	.335	.512
Personal Discrimination							
Victim of Hate Crime				-.775			.656
Racially Discriminated				-.681			.563
Church Membership						-.875	.800
Eigenvalue [c]	3.70	1.46	1.23	1.10	1.08	1.03	
Variance (%)	23.1	9.1	7.7	6.9	6.8	6.4	

Source: The Los Angeles Times Poll # 267 released through the Roper Center for Public Opinion Research.

[a] Loading scores greater than .30 or smaller than -.30.

[b] A communality in factor analysis shows how much variance of an observed variable is accounted for by the common factor. It is calculated by summing the squared factor loadings of a variable.

[c] An eigenvalue indicates how much of the variation in the original group of variables is accounted for by a particular factor.

from those influencing one's alienation from the dominant culture, but that there is *not* a zero-sum relationship between acculturation and ethnic attachment or mainstream detachment.

Consistent with findings in the previous chapter, the four indicators of group consciousness can be broken down into two dimensions —perception of group deprivation and personal experience of discrimination. However, both dimensions now have negative coefficients indicating that forces explaining the forging of the dimensions of acculturation, ethnic attachment, and mainstream detachment are likely to be negatively related to the formation of group consciousness. This is different from the principal component findings for Asian American panethnicity (Tables 3-2 and 3-3) where the dimension of group deprivation has an opposite sign to the dimension of personal discrimination.

For multiple regression analysis, a summed index of acculturation is created by taking the average of the six indicators (i.e., language use, media use, English fluency, speaking with whites, business contacts, and crossracial friendship; alpha=.83). Because of the lack of additivity for each of the other dimensions as indicated by their low alpha values, only variables with the top absolute loading coefficient in each dimension (i.e., preserve culture, expect to return, racism main barrier, victim of hate crime) plus intermarriage are entered in the following analysis.

RESULTS FROM MULTIPLE REGRESSION ANALYSIS

What explains the political integration at the individual level for Koreans in Los Angeles? Table 5-3 lists the results from three models of participation. In the basic socioeconomic model, having a higher level of education, more income, and being employed can all be positively related to one's likelihood to become registered voters. This appears to be in sharp contrast to the findings of the comparable models for the Asian sample in Tables 4-5 to 4-7 where education is the only socioeconomic variable to be associated with greater participation (turnout for citizens). However, the significance of socioeconomic factors disappears with the addition of demographic factors measuring one's length of stay, age, gender, and place of education.

In a manner consistent with Converse's (1969) speculation, length of stay for this group of Korean immigrants is a much more powerful predictor of participation than age.[2] Again, this finding diverts greatly

Table 5-3
Multiple Regression Estimations of the Political Participation of Koreans in
Los Angeles, 1992 (N=541)

Models	I	II	III
(1) Socioeconomic			
Education	.066*	.036	.030
	(.032)	(.026)	(.026)
Income	.137***	.036	.026
	(.027)	(.023)	(.023)
Employed	.216*	.082	-.031
	(.109)	(.089)	(.089)
(2) Demographic			
Length of Stay		.103***	.091***
		(.007)	(.007)
Age		-.066	-.044
		(.038)	(.040)
US Education		.210*	.118
		(.099)	(.101)
Female		-.113	-.199*
		(.076)	(.077)
(3) Socio-psychological			
Group Deprivation			.169
			(.074)
Personal Discrimination			-.125
			(.090)
Attachment to Ethnic Culture			.045
			(.066)
Church Membership			.055
			(.082)
Detachment from Mainstream			-.315**
			(.095)
Support Intermarriage			.088***
			(.025)
Acculturation			.178**
			(.064)
Constant	.053	-.108	-.695
	(.181)	(.194)	(.346)
Adjusted R^2	.104	.435	.472
F	21.93	60.43	35.41

Source: (see Table 5-2)
Note: The dependent variable is scored 3 if respondent is registered to vote. It is scored 2 if respondent is naturalized but not registered. It is scored 1 if respondent is not naturalized but expects to become so in the next few years. * $p<.05$ ** $p<.01$ *** $p<.001$
Numerical entries are unstandardized regression coefficients except where noted. Standard errors are in parentheses.

from that for the five groups of Asians. It is possible that, for the foreign-born generation alone, length of stay in a new country conveys more information than that of age in terms of one's potential for participation. This proposition, nevertheless, is not supported by analyzing only the foreign-born Asians in the Southern California survey (not shown) where length of stay has no impact on indicators of participation when age and other variables are controlled. This leads one to speculate that perhaps it is not nativity or immigration generation per se, but being of Korean origin that separates the role length of stay plays in Asian American and Korean immigrant participation.

When other sociodemographic variables are controlled, a Korean who has attended school in the States may be more likely to become a registered voter, and being female does not seem to be associated with less integration. The relationship between gender and participation is reversed when socio-psychological factors underlying the construction of ethnic identity are controlled. This finding of the net negative effect of being Korean and female is contrary to the net insignificant role of gender among Asians in the Southern California study. This indicates that, regarding political integration, Korean-born women may not be so much disadvantaged in socioeconomic and demographic backgrounds as in ethnic group identity and consciousness.

Besides being female, one's detachment from the host country and return to the homeland can also be associated with less integration. But a Korean who is more acculturated and supportive of intermarriage is more likely to become politically integrated. None of the other socio-psychological factors matter much for political integration except the perception of group deprivation (seeing racism as a barrier to success), which has a borderline significance (p=.07). This again differs from the findings among Asians in the Southern California survey taken 18 months after the Riots (Tables 4-6, 4-7) where being a victim of a hate crime can be associated with greater participation in activities other than voting and where gender does not matter. Nevertheless, the two surveys share the common finding that those who register or vote may be more likely to perceive group deprivation and support intermarriage. These commonalities and differences in the meanings and roles of ethnicity in immigrant political participation demonstrate vividly the situational and complex nature of the adaptation process.

Across the models, the explanatory power jumps from .10 to .44 when length of stay and place of education are taken into consideration. It continues to improve with the addition of certain socio-psychological factors, but the difference in the R-square is much smaller and place of education no longer matters much. This implies that length of stay is the strongest factor of all in relation to the extent of Korean American integration into the U.S. political system, followed by indicators of cultural and social adaptation as well as gender. By comparison, basic socioeconomic status, group consciousness, ethnic attachment, and church membership matter little.[3]

SUMMARY

The chapter begins by asking if a similar concept of ethnicity and its relationship to participation can be found when we focus attention on a group of Asian immigrants from Korea rather than on the composite Asian sample discussed in Chapter 4. Although the two surveys are not comparable in many ways, they both indicate that the structure of ethnicity is multifaceted and that one's being more acculturated does not necessarily lead to his/her being less concerned with ethnic group interests or the preservation of culture. In addition, both indicate that socioeconomic status has little to do with political participation when demographic and socio-psychological factors underlying the structure of ethnicity are controlled. However, the fact that variables such as age, length of stay, gender, and being a victim of a hate crime may each have a different relationship to political integration for the Asian respondents in the two surveys is sufficient evidence to call for more research.

Table 5-4
A Simplified Multiple Regression Model of the Political Participation of
Koreans in Los Angeles, 1992 (N=548)

Education	.025
	(.032)
Income	.030
	(.021)
Length of Stay	.087***
	(.006)
US Education	.155
	(.088)
Female	-.175*
	(.074)
Group Deprivation	.166
	(.094)
Detachment from Mainstream	-.305**
	(.094)
Support Intermarriage	.084***
	(.025)
Acculturation	.193**
	(.058)
Constant	-.154
	(.188)
Adjusted R^2	.472
F	55.23

Source and *Note:* (see Table 5-3)

NOTES

1. This figure, however, may reflect a gross undercount due to sampling bias, misclassification, and the systematic omission of certain persons of Korean origin (Yu 1982).

2. The impact of age here is measured in terms of five age groups. Their distribution is reported in Table 5-1. The findings are virtually the same when raw age is used, except that the coefficients for age are much smaller. The control for one's being older in age (over 65) is highly insignificant and the exclusion of it does not change findings. Another variation indexing the impact of time, i.e., percentage of political life in the United States (length/age), is significant but the overall explanatory power of the models is smaller than that using length of stay.

3. This is confirmed in a trimmed-down model of participation (Table 5-4) where every variable that has not shown any closeness to significance is removed one at a time under the condition that the relationship among other variables in the fuller model remains the same and the F-score for the reduced model gets larger.

CHAPTER 6

Does (Under-)Participation Matter?

An important concern in democratic politics is the meaning of participation. Scholars generally agree that there are three normative values of participation: legitimacy, instrumentalism, and self-development (Bennett and Resnick 1990). Participation, first of all, is assumed to enable the system's legitimacy and stability by establishing a link between public opinion and public policy. Second, participation can promote representation by giving citizens a say in the decisions of public policies. Third, participation may facilitate the development of deliberative and moral character which is intrinsic to democratic citizenship.

In recent decades, with the trend of declining voting turnout in American politics, the empirical effects of nonparticipation have been pushed to center stage. Ironically, except for the findings that nonvoters tend to have lower socioeconomic status and are slightly more liberal on domestic economic policies, little significant difference has been found between voters and nonvoters on the issues of public policy (Wolfinger and Rosenstone 1980; Shaffer 1982; Bennett and Resnick 1990; Petrocik and Shaw 1991; Gant and Lyons 1992; Teixeira 1992; Verba, Lehman, Schlozman, Brady, and Nie 1993a). However, it may be premature to conclude that nonparticipation does not matter.

In their seminal work on political participation and social equality, Verba and Nie (1972) note that although leaders may be considered responsive by adopting the same agenda for community action as that of the citizenry, their level of responsiveness is much higher in communities where participation rates are higher. Compared to other communities where participation rates are lower, there is also a wider gap of perceived government responsiveness between active and inactive citizens within these proactive communities. In a study conducted two decades later, Verba and his associates (1993a) again find participation, especially in activities beyond voting, to matter. Those whose preferences and needs become visible to policymakers through participatory activities are observed to differ from their more quiescent counterparts in their demographic attributes, economic needs, and the government benefits they receive.

Does (under-)participation matter for respondents of Asian origin? This is a logical concern following the discussions on the levels and determinants of Asian American participation. After all, the low level of participation of Asian Americans may not be as severe a concern if participants differ little from nonparticipants in terms of sociodemographic outlook and political orientations. However, for Asians—or any other racial or ethnic group that has a significant proportion of the foreign-born—the issue of nonvoting is complicated by one additional involuntary factor: Noncitizens are prohibited by law from registering to vote, even though they may perform the same levels of economic and political activities outside the voting booth as do citizens.[1] It follows that for Asians, participation in activities other than voting may not necessarily signify a higher level of political activism. For even though participation in activities such as contacting officials, making campaign contributions, attending meetings and the sort may demand more time, money, and/or skills and thus be more "difficult" than voting, these kinds of participatory activities are actually more *accessible* than voting *to* a large segment of the community members who are noncitizens.[2] This is one instance that demonstrates that the nature of low or no participation and its implications may be different for Asian Americans than for the American electorate as a whole (such as presented by the National Election Studies Series).

Further, particularly for communities where a significant proportion of the population are recent immigrants, the value of active participation in American politics is not without controversy. An author points out that the "allegiant and nonparticipatory disposition of the first generation insulates the United States from the ideological dissonance that immigrants portend" and helps promote democratic stability (Harles 1993, 206). This resonates Berelson, Lazarsfeld, and McPhee's (1954) view that "the apathetic segment of America probably has helped to hold the system together and cushioned the shock of disagreement, adjustment and change" (322). This view may also be derived from the disputable assumption that recent foreign-born immigrants hold different and anti-democratic political orientations than the native-born.

In this chapter, Asian American participation in various types of electoral activities and their policy ramifications are examined in the aggregate using selected items in the six-county survey of Southern Californians. The analysis compares the sociodemographic outlook, immigrant minority group experience, information level, and political orientations and choices between participants and nonparticipants within the Asian sample. In addition, it compares the opinions of Asian voters to the opinions of black, Latino, and non-Hispanic white voters in the survey. Further, it examines the degree of racial disparity between voters and nonvoters in terms of policy opinions and other political orientations.

THE ISSUES

The four policy issues examined in this chapter are: (1) affirmative action in college admissions, (2) temporary restriction of legal immigration, (3) asylum hearings in illegal immigration, and (4) reparations for Japanese Americans. (Exact question wording of survey items used are reported in section IV of Appendix D). These issues concerning immigration, civil liberties, and civil rights were selected not only because opinions toward them are tallied in the Southern California survey, but because they have been and remain important public policy concerns for both Asian and non-Asian residents of a community experiencing rapid social and political changes.

The issue of affirmative action in higher education is of particular concern to many Asians because of suspected discrimination practiced by a number of leading institutions including the University of California at Berkeley and at Los Angeles against Asian applicants. Many report that highly-qualified Asians are denied admission into these institutions because of concerns about the overrepresentation of Asians as well as the existence of racial quotas reserved for other minorities. Although the situation of Asians is central to the shifting discourse ocntemplating a retreat from civil rights concerns for other minorities (Takagi 1992), mass opinions among Asians and in comparison to other groups have not been systematically examined.

Although most Californians relate the issue of illegal immigration to undocumented Mexicans arriving from south of the Border, periodic attempts by Asians to enter the United States via the ocean have also been widely reported in the news. Weeks before the August 1993 survey, three ships transporting over six hundred Chinese nationals were intercepted by the U.S. Coast Guard and kept in international waters. The Associated Press reported on July 16, 1993 that U.S. authorities had reached an agreement with the Mexican government to take the Chinese so that they would not be eligible to apply for political asylum in the United States, a process that often takes years. The decision to preempt asylum hearings to the Chinese occurred at a time when election-minded top California state officials seized the event to blame immigrants, legal or not, for economic and social problems. Governor Wilson in particular attributed the state's economic woes to unfunded federal immigration policies. In this anti-immigrant environment, any proposal to restrict immigration became an appealing panacea, and Asian immigrants, like Asian students, became a ploy in the debate over public policies.

The civil liberties and constitutional rights of 112,000 Japanese Americans residing on the West Coast were violated during World War II because of racism, wartime hysteria, and political/economic concerns (Commission on Wartime Relocation and Internment of Civilians 1982). Although a bill rewarding reparations to surviving internees were signed into law in 1988 through the remarkable efforts led by Japanese American community organizations, members in Congress, and the internees themselves, the issues of appropriations and expansion of coverage were separate battles encumbered by the concerns over the federal budget deficits (Hatamiya 1993). Moreover, heightened demands for reparations also came from African Americans whose "40 acres and a mule" promised by Union General William Sherman have yet to be delivered. Nevertheless, the Japanese American redress movement continued to thrive. On August 4, 1993, the U.S. Justice Department agreed to pay $20,000 apiece to 73 Japanese Americans born in internment camps to women who had left but returned to camps during their pregnancy for support from family members still kept behind the barbed wires (Jung 1993). However, not all local residents of the Southern California community, who were being inundated by public officials' expressive concerns over the state economy and nonwhite immigration, were able to stand firmly behind the principles of civil rights and liberties underlying the issues of reparations for Japanese Americans.

THE MEANING OF PARTICIPATION AMONG ASIAN AMERICANS

Among Asian Americans surveyed, how much do voters differ from nonvoters in terms of sociodemographic attributes? In the micro-level analysis presented in chapter 4, Asians who are older and have higher family incomes are more likely to register and vote when other variables are controlled. The aggregate-level results comparing the percentage distributions for those who voted to those who did not in the 1992 Presidential election (columns 1 and 2 of Table 6-1) convey a similar, if not sharper, sociodemographic disparity in turnout. Like the American electorate in general, voters of Asian origin tend to be more highly educated, well-off, native-born, older, and to have lived for a longer time in the Southern California community than their nonvoting counterparts. A parallel observation can be made between voting and nonvoting citizens (columns 1 and 3), except that education and income now appear to have stronger relationships to voting than do other indicators of sociodemographic background. This differs from the previous case when noncitizens are involved in the comparison, where demographic variables such as length of stay and age have higher Kendall's tau-c[3] values.

The sociodemographic distinctions involving participation in activities other than voting are much less conspicuous (columns 4 and 5). In fact, the various tests of association indicate that differences in education, income, nativity, length of stay, and age do not seem to matter much in terms of participation. However, the higher percentages of the well-off and the unemployed among participants seem to indicate that those having more money or more time may be more likely to participate in activities such as contacting officials, donating money, attending meetings, or volunteering for a political course. These results both resemble and depart from findings surveying the American public as a whole. Like other Americans, the participation of Asian Americans may be a function of socioeconomic status. Unlike the predominnatly white participants studied by Verba and his associates (1993a), Asian participants possess a socioeconomic profile closer to nonparticipants than do Asian voters to nonvoters.

Some suspect that nonparticipation in electoral politics may be an indication of political discontent. However, although nonvoters have been found to be more dissatisfied than being uninformed or indifferent (Ragsdale and Rusk 1993), and political discontent may motivate participation in unconventional activities such as sit-ins, boycotts, and protests (Citrin 1977), there has been little empirical evidence that nonvoters are less supportive of democratic ideals or feel more alienated than voters do (Kinder and Sears 1985; Bennett and Resnick 1990). When feelings of alienation and discontent are measured in terms of experiences of discrimination and perceptions of group deprivation, the results (Table 6-2) indicate that Asian voters are more likely to experience some form of

Table 6-1
Percentage Differences between Asian American Participants and
Nonparticipants in Terms of Sociodemographic Background

	Voting		Other Participation		Difference
	Yes	No	Yes	No	
	(1)	(2)(3)	(4)	(5)	(1)-(4)
Base N	81	140(73)ᵃ	54	167	

Sociodemographic Background
Education

< High School	7%	20%(17%)	13%	16%	-6%
> College Degree	64	45 (38)	52	52	12
	χ^2=11.40(12.98*)		χ^2=1.09	df=6	
	t_c=.19**(.32**)		t_c=.02		

Family Income

< $20K	5	23 (16)	17	15	-12
> $60K	43	23 (24)	40	27	3
	χ^2=22.24**(14.89*)		χ^2=6.95	df=6	
	t_c=.25**(.28**)		t_c=.05		

Unemployment	10	11 (6)	15	9	-5
	n.s.	(n.s.)	n.s		

Foreign-born	37	61 (47)	50	53	-13
	χ^2=11.53**(1.44)		n.s.	df=1	

Length of Stay

< 5 years	10	27 (12)	15	22	-5
>20 years	53	22 (37)	35	33	18
	χ^2=31.14**(6.35)		χ^2=3.75	df=6	
	t_c=.38**(.19*)		t_c=.04		

Male	51	53 (41)	48	53	3
	n.s.	(n.s.)	n.s.		

Age (18-24)	22	31 (28)	23	29	-6
(25-39)	30	45 (41)	42	38	-12
(65+)	11	5 (7)	6	8	5
	χ^2=16.99**(8.44)		χ^2=2.33	df=5	
	t_c=.24**(.19*)		t_c=.05		

Source: The Los Angeles Times Poll #318, August 7-10, 1993, released through the Roper
Center for Public Opinion Research.
ᵃEntries in parentheses are those among nonvoting citizens.*p<.05 **p<.005

Table 6-2

Percentage Differences between Asian American Participants and
Nonparticipants in Terms of Minority Group Experience and Information Level

	Voting		Other Participation		Difference
	Yes	No	Yes	No	
	(1)	(2)(3)	(4)	(5)	(1)-(4)
Base N	81	140(73)[a]	54	167	

Minority Group Experience
Personal Experience of Discrimination

Great Deal	5%	2%(4%)	7%	7%	-2%
Fair Amount	10	9 (12)	7	10	3
Some Amount	57	47 (45)	63	47	-6
None	28	41 (38)	22	41	6
	χ^2=4.61 (2.42)		χ^2=10.57*	df=3	
	t_c=.13* (.08)		t_c=.15*		

Victim of Hate Crime	18	18 (17)	32	13	-14
	n.s. (n.s.)		χ^2=9.46** df=1		
Hear Racial Slurs About Asians					
Very Often	13	11 (8)	13	11	0
Fairly Often	14	15 (13)	19	13	-5
Fairly Infrequent	33	22 (22)	32	24	1
Very Infrequent	41	53 (57)	37	52	4
	χ^2=4.00 (4.38)		χ^2=3.69	df=3	
	t_c=.09 (.16)		t_c=.11		

Group Most Deprived	19	18 (11)	17	19	2
	n.s. (n.s.)		n.s.		
Group Condition Bad	10	11 (10)	19	8	-9
	n.s. (n.s.)		χ^2=5.38	df=3	

Dissatisfaction	10	19 (25)	19	15	9
	χ^2=3.01 (6.16*)		n.s.	df=1	
Information Level					
Know Group Leaders	52	30 (30)	39	38	13
	χ^2=10.40**(7.45**)		n.s.	df=1	

Know Group History	62	48 (55)	57	52	5
	χ^2=3.96* (.76)		n.s.	df=1	

Know of Internment	92	87 (87)	92	89	0
	n.s. (n.s.)		n.s.		

Note: (see Table 6-1)

discrimination than nonvoters in the Asian sample. Among citizens, they also hear more frequently of racial slurs made against their panethnic group and perceive Asians as the most deprived minority group.

A slightly different pattern emerges in comparisons involving participation in activities other than voting. Although participants are slightly more likely to hear more frequently of racial slurs[4] and to perceive their group condition as being relatively worse off than are nonparticipants in the Asian sample, they are far more likely to experience discrimination and to be victimized by hate crimes. These results seem to suggest that in the aggregate the source of Asian nonparticipation, particularly in activities other than voting, has little to do with the feelings of alienation; rather, it has more to do with the experience of racial group discrimination.

The above observation, however, is not equivalent to saying that Asian nonvoters or nonparticipants are more content with the current political or social situation. In fact, when discontent is measured in terms of dissatisfaction with life in the Southern Californian community, the message is to the contrary. Nonvoters, especially those that are citizens, express a much higher dissatisfaction with life than voters. Although those who participate in other activities tend to be more dissatisfied than the less active, the between group difference does not reach statistical significance. This suggests that most Asian American respondents do not seem to link grievances in their personal life with group position in the socio-political system nor, when eligible, seek redress through voting.

Information level may be another factor separating participants from nonparticipants. Many studies find that nonvoters across the board are more politically ignorant than voters (Bennett and Resnick 1990). This seems to be true with this sample of Asians. A significantly higher percentage of Asian voters can name at least one prominent group political leader than can their non-voting counterparts. The gap between voters and nonvoters shrinks sharply, though, in terms of knowing the length of group history and the incidence of the Japanese internment during WWII. Nor do nonparticipants possess a lower level of information than participants on these matters. In fact, more than eight out of ten respondents, including nonparticipants, are aware of the internment of Japanese Americans that happened over a half century ago.

Do differences in sociodemographic background, minority group experience, and information level have any bearing on policy preferences? The answer appears to be negative when the opinions of voters are compared to those of nonvoters on three of the four issues examined

(Table 6-3). Within the Asian sample, voters appear to be more supportive of admissions based on racial makeup than merit. Their opinion seems to be more polarized on the issue of banning legal immigration for three years. But the differences are small and do not reach any statistical significance. However, on awarding reparation payments to the Japanese Americans confined in internment camps during World War II, a much higher percentage of voters are more strongly supportive of the policy. Since this issue deals mostly with the interests of a subgroup, the pattern discussed above suggests that voters, being more integrated, may be more likely to link sub-group interests with pan-group interests. Yet, the size of the difference also indicates that policy representation may become an issue when controversies perceived to benefit only one segment of the panethnic community arise.

Conversely, few of the policy preferences of survey respondents involved in activities other than voting can be said to mirror those of the nonparticipants. On the issue of college admission, participants tend to be more supportive of admissions based on merit than on racial makeup. On banning legal immigration for three years, participants are more likely to oppose the idea. A similar pattern exists regarding the issue of not granting asylum hearings to Chinese boat people, where a much higher percentage of participants strongly oppose the refusal. However, the difference in the support for reparations between participants and nonparticipants is statistically insignificant.

Why is there such a disparity in the representation of issue concerns between voters and participants? Besides what has been discussed earlier that the nature and requirements for voting are different from those of participation in activities other than voting for many members of this immigrant group, part of the answer may be provided by comparing voters and participants along a number of categories in terms of percentage distributions (last column of Tables 6-1 to 6-3). Compared to voters, participants are generally less educated, less well-off, younger, and more likely to be unemployed, foreign-born, and have a shorter length of stay than voters. They often experience greater amounts of abuse and discrimination and perceive their group condition as wanting. They are also less able to name group political leaders.

The source of the divergence between the efficacy of issue representation for the two types of activists may also be attributed to the differences in political ideology and the perceived public support for Asian candidates. Compared to nonvoters, voters tend to be more conservative and see no difference between Asian candidates and those

Table 6-3

Percentage Differences Between Asian American Participants and
Nonparticipants in Terms of Policy Preferences and Other Political
Orientations

	Voting		Other Participation		Difference
	Yes	No	Yes	No	
	(1)	(2)	(3)	(4) (5)	(1)-(4)
Base N	81	140(73)[a]	54	167	

Policy Preferences
College Admission

Admit by Merit	75%	79%(79%)	85%	75%	-10%
Mirror Makeup	24	18 (20)	15	22	9
	χ^2=.87	(.39)	χ^2=1.34		
	t_c=.05	(.04)	t_c=-.08		

Ban Legal Immigration

Favor Strongly	25	19 (26)	14	24	11
Favor Somewhat	20	23 (25)	25	21	-5
Oppose Somewhat	25	31 (28)	21	31	4
Oppose Strongly	30	27 (22)	40	24	-10
	χ^2=1.73	(1.51)	χ^2=7.58*	df=3	
	t_c=.01	(-.08)	t_c=-.14		

No Asylum Hearing

Approve Strongly	40	43 (42)	37	44	3
Approve Somewhat	21	19 (20)	16	21	5
Oppose Somewhat	13	16 (19)	8	17	5
Oppose Strongly	25	22 (20)	39	18	-14
	χ^2= .64	(1.06)	χ^2=9.40	df=3	
	t_c=-.03	(-.03)	t_c=-.12		

Award Reparations

Approve Strongly	73	50 (52)	67	56	6
Approve Somewhat	16	34 (33)	23	29	-7
Oppose Somewhat	3	8 (6)	0	8	3
Oppose Strongly	8	8 (9)	10	8	-2
	χ^2=11.37**(7.33)		χ^2=5.11	df=3	
	t_c=.20**	(.19*)	t_c=.08		

Table 6-3—Continued

	Voting		Other Participation		Difference
	Yes	No	Yes	No	
	(1)	(2)	(3)	(4) (5)	(1)-(4)
Base N	81	140(73)[a]	54	167	

Political Ideology

Very Liberal	6	7 (4)	8	6	-2
Somewhat Liberal	20	25 (26)	32	21	-12
Middle	29	28 (36)	21	31	8
Somewhat Conserv.	34	25 (24)	26	29	8
Very Conservative	6	8 (7)	9	7	-3
No Attention	4	6 (3)	4	6	0
	χ_v^2=2.61 (2.54)		χ^2=4.59	df=5	
	t_c=.08 (.07)		t_c=-05		

Perceived Vote for Asian Candidates

Prefer Asian	8	7 (6)	8	7	0
No Difference	60	47 (46)	48	53	12
Uncomfortable	32	47 (48)	44	40	-12
	χ^2=4.08 (3.46)		χ^2=.37	df=2	
	t_c=.14* (.16)		t_c=-.02		

Note: (see Table 6-1)

from other panethnic groups. Those who participate in activities other than voting, on the other hand, tend to be more liberal and more pessimistic about others' likelihood to vote for Asian candidates when compared either to nonparticipants or to voters. Interestingly, this latter type of opinion pattern is very similar to that of nonvoters, where there is an even larger share of respondents who feel other people are uncomfortable with Asian candidates. The lack of perceived benefit (prospect of winning) may be an important factor explaining the lack of voting participation by Asian Americans observed in the present study.[5]

THE MEANING OF ASIAN PARTICIPATION IN A COMPARATIVE PERSPECTIVE

The meaning of Asian American political participation can also be indicated by the uniqueness of policy preferences and political orientations expressed by Asian voters. As shown in Table 6-4, as far as the four policy issues are concerned, Asian voters hold a very different policy outlook than voters of other groups. Compared to non-Asian groups, more Asian voters support college admissions based on merit and the awarding of reparations to Japanese Americans, and fewer Asian voters support proposals to ban legal immigration and to send back Chinese boat people without asylum hearings. The greatest difference in opinions occurs between Asian and black voters, particularly on the issue of reparations where 40% more Asian voters support the policy. Smaller differences are found between Asian and Latino voters on the two immigration issues—banning immigration and no asylum hearings—where t-tests for differences in group mean fail to reject the null hypothesis of no difference. Although the mean of opinions between white and Asian voters differ much across all four issues, white voters most resemble Asian voters in their attitude toward the criterion of college admission.

These crossracial patterns provide indications of the prospects for and obstacles to the forming of intergroup coalitions. They show that in the intricate multiethnic environment of Southern California there may be no lasting coalition partner for Asians. Depending on the issues involved, Asians may have to form different biracial or multiracial coalitions. On issues concerning immigration, Latinos are the most likely partners. On issues concerning civil rights, Asians may have closer views to whites than to others.[6] And on the issue of reparations for past injuries done to the civil liberties of a minority group, blacks are ironically the least likely

Table 6-4
Percentage Difference Between Voters and Nonvoters in Terms of Policy and
Other Orientations Across Four Panethnic Groups

	Asian	Latino	Black	White
College Admission				
Admit by Merit	75%(79%)[a]	52%(35%)	44%(33%)	64%(59%)
Mirror Makeup	24 (18)	38 (56)	53 (58)	30 (35)
Neither	1 (2)	10 (9)	3 (10)	7 (6)
N=	79(125)	71(106)	89(40)	438(175)
	$\chi^2=.87^b$	$\chi^2=5.74*$	$\chi^2=.61^b$	$\chi^2=2.05$
	$t_c=.05$	$t_c=-.15*$	$t_c=-.07$	$t_c=-.03$
T-test for Group Means	$t_{AL}=3.84$	$t_{AB}=4.10$	$t_{AW}=2.36$	
Ban Immigration				
Favor Strongly	25 (19)	32 (29)	54 (50)	47 (45)
Favor Somewhat	20 (23)	22 (21)	24 (21)	15 (19)
Oppose Somewhat	25 (31)	19 (21)	9 (7)	20 (16)
Oppose Strongly	30 (27)	28 (29)	14 (21)	19 (20)
N=	76(124)	69(117)	93(42)	439(173)
	$\chi^2=1.73$	$\chi^2=.32$	$\chi^2=1.20$	$\chi^2=2.54$
	$t_c=.01$	$t_c=.04$	$t_c=.06$	$t_c=.01$
T-test for Group Means	$t_{AL}=.94$	$t_{AB}=4.49$	$t_{AW}=3.42$	
No Asylum Hearing				
Approve Strongly	40 (43)	51 (39)	60 (60)	60 (60)
Approve Somewhat	21 (19)	9 (12)	11 (17)	18 (9)
Oppose Somewhat	13 (16)	13 (21)	6 (17)	8 (12)
Oppose Strongly	25 (22)	28 (29)	23 (7)	15 (19)
N=	75(122)	69(111)	91(42)	441(176)
	$\chi^2=.64$	$\chi^2=3.21$	$\chi^2=8.75*$	$\chi^2=10.73*$
	$t_c=-.03$	$t_c=.09$	$t_c=-.04$	$t_c=.02$
T-test for Group Means	$t_{AL}=.76$	$t_{AB}=1.69$	$t_{AW}=3.29$	

[a]Entries in parentheses are those of nonvoting respondents including noncitizens.
[b]Response category with the smallest frequency is excluded.

Table 6-4-Continued

	Asian	Latino	Black	White
Award Reparations				
Favor Strongly	73%(50%)	44%(39%)	33%(30%)	44%(36%)
Favor Somewhat	16 (34)	28 (30)	18 (15)	24 (32)
Oppose Somewhat	3 (8)	13 (15)	14 (15)	12 (14)
Oppose Strongly	8 (8)	16 (16)	35 (40)	20 (18)
N=	74 (120)	69(107)	87(40)	442(170)
	χ^2=11.37**	χ^2=.37	χ^2=.53	χ^2=5.71
	t_c=.20**	t_c=.04	t_c=.06	t_c=.04
T-test for Group Means	t_{AL}=-3.31	t_{AB}=-5.86	t_{AW}=-4.36	
Political Ideology				
Very Liberal	6 (7)	9 (16)	12 (16)	6 (10)
Somewhat Lib.	20 (25)	29 (10)	26 (23)	21 (19)
Middle	29 (28)	29 (24)	32 (26)	30 (32)
Somewhat Cons.	34 (25)	29 (28)	19 (26)	30 (28)
Very Conserv.	6 (8)	4 (14)	10 (5)	13 (9)
No Attention	4 (6)	1 (9)	2 (5)	1 (2)
N=	79(134)	70(118)	95(43)	453(183)
	χ^2=2.61	χ^2=18.49**	χ^2=3.11	χ^2=6.76
	t_c=.08	t_c=-.04	t_c=.05	t_c=.06
T-test for Group Means	t_{AL}=-.82	t_{AB}=-1.12	t_{AW}=1.24	
Perceived Vote for Asian Candidates				
Prefer Asian	8 (7)	3 (8)	5 (5)	3 (4)
No Difference	60 (47)	68 (54)	51 (43)	71 (62)
Uncomfortable	32 (41)	29 (39)	44 (51)	26 (34)
N=	72(122)	68(104)	86(37)	422(168)
	χ^2=4.08	χ^2=3.88	χ^2=1.85[b]	χ^2=4.71
	t_c=.14*	t_c=.05	t_c=.12	t_c=.06
T-test for Group Means	t_{AL}=.50	t_{AB}=1.36	t_{AW}=-1.58	

Source: (see Table 6-1)
[a]Entries in parentheses are those of nonvoting respondents including noncitizens.
[b]Response category with the smallest frequency is excluded.

supporters of this policy which so far is believed to have only benefitted Japanese Americans.

When the extent of discrepancy in policy opinions between Asian voters and nonvoters is compared to that for each of the three other racial/ethnic groups, there is a striking degree of similarity on the surface. Although Asian voters hold a very different policy outlook from non-Asian voters, in each group they all differ little from their nonvotingcounterparts in most of the policy items examined. This seems to suggest support for the idea that there is no immediate ground for concern over the issue of nonvoting. Yet, neither is there a common issue cleavage when concerns of voters of divergent racial backgrounds do depart from their nonvoting counterparts.

The issue that divides Asian voters and nonvoters, as discussed earlier, is the rewarding of reparations to Japanese American internees. For Latinos, a significant source of division comes from the criterion of college admission. While more voters support admission on merit, more than half of the nonvoters support the more affirmative action option. An equal proportion of both black and non-Hispanic white voters and nonvoters strongly support the denial of asylum hearings to the illegal Chinese immigrants. Yet, more black voters are opposed strongly to the denial of legal procedures than black nonvoters. This again differs from the more disparate pattern among whites. The greatest extent of diversion in issue opinions between voters and nonvoters lies, however, in the opinion towards reparations among Asians. This implies that for an emerging minority group such as Asians, those who are more integrated into the political system may be more likely to hold a different issue agenda than the nonvoting segment of the multiethnic community. Hence, the issue of policy representation through voting should be of greater concern to Asians than to other groups.

The role Asian American voters play in shaping ethnic politics in Southern California can be further clarified by examining the distribution of political ideology and the perceived electoral support for Asian candidates. Compared to voters of other racial backgrounds, Asians are most similar to whites in terms of ideological outlook—though the percentage of the very conservative is higher among whites and the percentage of those paying no attention to ideology is higher among Asians. Although about the same percentage of voters in both Asian and Latino groups express a conservative orientation, Latino voters as a group are generally more liberal than Asians. In terms of between-group means, however, Asians voters do not differ significantly in ideology from their non-Asian counterparts. Within each group, the ideological difference between voters and nonvoters is also negligible except for the Latinos where nonvoters hold either more extreme or no ideological preferences.

On the perception of others' likelihood to vote for Asian candidates, Asian voters do not seem to express as much confidence in their own candidates as non-Hispanic whites or Latinos do. Although a higher percentage of Asians believe others might prefer Asian candidates, the size is very small. On the other hand, about one third of Asian voters think others would feel uncomfortable voting for Asians. This is higher than the percentage among Latinos or whites. Relatedly, Asian voters are trailed only by black voters in terms of the perception of no difference between Asian candidates and those of other races. Nevertheless, none of the tests for equality of between-group means reach statistical significance at .05 level. The good news here for prospective Asian candidates is that within each racial group the percentage of no difference is much larger than those stating uneasiness. Although the perception of voters does not differ significantly from nonvoters in most groups, the disparity is greater inside the two newer immigrant groups (i.e., Asians and Latinos).

SUMMARY

Does participation matter for Asians? The answer here can only be a tentative one because of the limited number of policy items available. Yet, findings in this chapter suggest that Asian American political participation does matter and it may matter more for Asian Americans. However, there are important differences between participation in voting and in other election-related activities. In terms of voting, Asian participants, very much like American voters as a whole, are overrepresented in the higher socioeconomic class and posess more of a conservative political ideology. Compared to Asian nonvoters, they have a stronger sense of group consciousness arising from their personal experience of discrimination and perception of group deprivation, but they also express fewer grievances about personal life in Southern California and are more informed about group political leaders. Asian participants in activities other than voting are more similar in sociodemographic outlook to nonparticipants. They also share many characteristics of nonvoters. Compared to nonparticipants, they have more experiences of discrimination and are more dissatisfied with life. They are not more informed but do hold a very different policy agenda from the less active members. They are the more liberal segment of the Asian sample and, like nonvoters, feel others are uncomfortable with Asian candidates.

Although Asian voters do not differ much from nonvoters in terms of policy preferences, they are much more supportive of awarding reparations to Japanese Americans. Compared to other ethnic groups, the policy preferences of Asian voters are distinctive and this cannot be readily explained by political ideology. However, the combination of distinctive policy orientations with the wider divergence of opinions between voters and nonvoters indicates that through their participation in the American electoral system Asian voters may exert greater impact on the community agenda than voters in other groups.

Comparisons between participants and nonparticipants in terms of policy attitudes address, nonetheless, partly and indirectly the issue of representation. The selection of issues examined may be a source of bias. Several authors suggest that one may want to examine the policy-relevant context that shapes the needs and benefits of activists such as the circumstances of economic deprivation and dependence upon government programs (Verba et al. 1993a). The meaning of representation in minority politics also needs to be evaluated by the different policy outcomes for each of the communities (Button 1989). Last, investigations ought to be carried out comparing the level of concurrence between views expressed by community leaders and participants (Verba and Nie 1972). These are all suggested agendas for future research.

Besides the concern over democratic representation, the values of Asian American participation in American politics can also be underscored in terms of the meanings of the acts themselves. To the extent that political participation is an act in support of government and politics, more integration into the U.S. political system for those with recent immigration backgrounds through citizenship and voting may help to deflect the discriminatory charges against immigrants. To the extent that political participation can influence the selection and/or the actions of government officials, more participation means better representation and more chances of gaining access and clout. Compared to national elections, the effect of more participation for Asians in local elections where turnout is usually very low may also loom larger than the size of the population would indicate (Cavanagh 1991). No matter how one chooses to look, it makes sense to promote more participation. In the next and last chapter, I will discuss the role some institutions play in meeting this challenge.

NOTES

1. This observation of no difference can be attested to by comparing the socioeconomic and participation indicators of Asian American citizens and noncitizens in the survey of Southern Californians. Of the three socioeconomic indicators (education, unemployment, and family income), the first two do not have significant Pearson Chi-square values at .05 level of significance. Neither do citizens and noncitizens differ much in terms of the extent and the likelihood of participation in activities other than voting.

2. According to census estimates shown in Appendix A, about 45% of voting-age Asians were noncitizens in the 1990s.

3. Kendall's tau-c is one of the measures of association between two ordinal variables. Tau-c is preferred to other ordinal measures of association for it can reach +/- 1.00 for table of any size. The absolute value should be closer to 1.00 if the degree of correlation is stronger between the two variables.

4. The frequency of hearing racial slurs may be a function of the respondent's English language proficiency. Unfortunately, there is no question in the survey to control for this possibility.

5. When this variable was added to the models reported in Chapter 4, the unstandardized coefficients for Asian American voting among citizens and participation among all respondents were not significant at the .05 level of significance (P=.37 for both). However, consistent with the hypothesized direction, the signs are both negative.

6. The issue of civil rights is a highly complex one and the study of opinion patterns on affirmative action in higher education can only tap a small aspect of it. More research is needed before a more conclusive remark concerning this issue can be made.

CHAPTER 7

Conclusion

The last three decades have witnessed an unprecedented tide of immigration to the United States from Asian and Latin American countries. Renewed concern over the negative impact of immigration increased to such an extent that in California a ballot initiative in the November 1994 mid-term election (Proposition 187) proposed to ban most public assistance to illegal immigrants and their children. The proposition passed by a large margin despite its possible violation of a federal law mandating public school education to all children residing in the United States; its potentially devastating effect on public health and social stability; and its explicit discriminatory effect which renders suspect more than one-third of the state's population identified in the 1990 Census as being of Asian or Hispanic descent. This was followed by the passage of the Personal Responsibilities Act in Congress and the California Civil Rights Initiative (Proposition 209) in 1996. This series of backlashes against immigrants and minorities illustrate the perilous condition and the lack of political clout of these groups. Focusing on persons originating from Asia, this study has examined the shape, the source, and the effect of political participation of Asian Americans as a group and as compared to other racial and ethnic groups in Southern California.

Much removed from the "sojourner" image of early Chinese immigrants, today's Asian Americans are touted as the "model minority"—a minority group that values family, education, hard work, and has achieved the highest overall level of socioeconomic success among all ethnic groups in recent decades. Yet, this emphasis on the amorphous "traditional culture" and the aggregated measure of socioeconomic status overlooks the lack of political participation and incorporation of this multiethnic minority group. The status of today's Asian Americans is in fact a bifurcated one. Underneath the facade of prosperity is widespread economic diversity among the different ethnic groups. Behind the impressive record of naturalization is the lack of progress in moving up the ladder of political integration through registration, voting, and election to important public offices. Although excessive political campaign contributions by some members of the panethnic community have been reported in the media, gross underrepresentation of Asians exists at every level of government.

Who is more likely to register and turn out to vote or participate in other election-related activities? What roles do socioeconomic status and other factors that are commonly related to the political participation of Asians play as compared to other racial/ethnic groups? To the extent that a panethnic group consciousness is valid and viable for Asians, this study asks whether and how much panethnic identity matters for political participation. Additionally, by comparing the meanings of panethnic and specific ethnic group identity, using Korean Americans as an example, the study aims to advance our understanding of the dynamics between ethnicity and political participation.

SUMMARY OF FINDINGS

What follows is a summary of major findings from the analysis of two *Los Angeles Times* surveys used in this study:

1. In contrast to Latinos or African Americans, Asian Americans evidence a participation deficit that cannot be explained away by the differences between non-Hispanic whites and Asians in socioeconomic status, demographic background, socio-psychological attitudes, and legal constraints. Indeed, the turnout and participation patterns of Asians become more of a puzzle when only socioeconomic status is controlled. Asian (pan)ethnicity does seem to matter for political participation. Yet, among the five major Asian groups studied, one's national or ethnic origin has little relationship to the probability of registration, voting, or the extent of participation in activities other than voting when other conditions are equal. Being a Korean in Los Angeles after the Rodney King Riots of 1992, on the other hand, does have a positive relationship to the likelihood of practicing some form of election-related activities besides voting.

2. Although socioeconomic status is not as useful a tool to predict the participation of Asian Americans as it is for other racial/ethnic groups, Asian American citizens with a higher family income have a greater

likelihood to register and/or to vote than those of lower income status. An Asian American's income, education, and employment status cannot be used, however, to shed any light on one's likelihood or the extent of participation in activities other than voting. Nor can they be used to explain the political integration of a sample of Korean-born respondents in Los Angeles. Partly because of the preponderance of an "odd" combination of relatively high socioeconomic status with very recent immigration history in today's Asian American population, the classic socioeconomic model of political participation observed in the more established and European-dominated groups cannot be generalized in a wholesale manner to explain the behaviors of Asians.

3. Similarly, the influence of demographic factors on political participation is comparatively weak for Asians. Yet, like the majority of the American electorate, being older can increase the probability of voter registration or voting among Asian American citizens. Length of stay, though weaker than age in predicting participation for Asians in general, is the single most powerful predictor of political integration for a group of Korean-born immigrants. The issue of gender arises in the finding that Korean immigrant women participate at a lower rate than their male counterparts even after controlling for a number of variables which may contribute to the differences between men and women.

4. The construction of ethnicity, cast either at the pan-group level or at the specific-group level, involves multidimensional processes. A model incorporating socio-psychological measures associated with these processes, though not sufficient to compensate for the participation disparity between Asians and non-Hispanic white Americans, is the most useful of all models in explaining the turnout and other participation of Asians. Being concerned over group status, perceiving Asians as the most deprived group, and giving support to intermarriage are associated with greater voting rates among citizens. Being victimized by hate crimes in the post-Rodney King era alone may increase the probability and extent of participation in activities other than voting. Among Korean-born Asians, being more acculturated and supportive of intermarriage may indicate greater integration, whereas being detached from the mainstream may discourage integration into the U.S. political system.

5. Although voters—regardless of racial group origin—do not differ much from nonvoters in their policy preferences, the nature of low or no participation and its implications on policy representation are different for Asians than for other groups. It matters if Asians participate and the issue of policy representation should be of greater concern to Asians than to

other groups. Because Asian voters have different outlooks and policy preferences from those Asian citizens and noncitizens who practice a more "active" approach to influencing politics, it also matters how one participates.

Mainstream political science methodology provides these answers to the questions of Asian American political participation both comparatively and internally. The results present for the first time an attempt to comprehend the dynamics between Asian American group identity and electoral participation at three levels—across panethnic groups, inside the pan-Asian group, and within a specific Asian ethnic group. Yet, judging from the persistent and negative coefficients for the pan-Asian group culture variable, the study, like two other studies on the same subject (i.e., Uhlaner, Cain, and Kiewiet 1989; Leighley and Vedlitz, 1994), fails to locate a generalized model of political participation for the four major racial/ethnic groups in the United States. Judging from the large number of insignificant variables in the Asian models, particularly those predicting participation beyond voting, it can be concluded that the factors influencing participation which structure the models of political participation derived from studying the American mainstream are not suitable for predicting or explaining the political behavior of Asian Americans.

On the one hand, the lack of "significant" findings may be a function of the omission of important variables that cannot be included in the analysis. The omitted variables that may significantly influence ethnic participation include, but are not limited to, political party affiliation, internal political efficacy and sense of civic duty, ethnic and nonethnic group membership, prior socialization experiences, and exposure to mainstream and ethnic media. It is also possible that the analyses fail to take into account certain systemic forces that work disproportionately against the group. These forces include the lack of Asian-dominated electoral districts and Asian candidates who can provide meaningful political competition and choices, as well as insufficient efforts by political parties and other agents of mobilization to establish an understanding of the democratic linkage between people and government among Asian Americans.

On the other hand, the lack of "significant" findings underscores the unique patterns of Asian American political participation, where even null findings have great implications for the source, shape, and impact of Asian participation. We learn, for instance, that the degree of political activism of the pan-Asian community may not be decided by any specific difference in immigration generation, length of stay, gender, income, education, employment status, or for the most part, ethnic group origin, when other conditions are equal. We also learn that citizenship and voter registration requirements, though effectively blocking a significant portion of Asians from turning out to vote, may not be sufficient in and of themselves to dictate the probability and extent of participation in activities other than voting among Asians.

Within a specific group of Asians, the Korean Americans, we learn that none of the indicators of socioeconomic status, age, and place of education can be a source of difference in the extent of political integration. Similar to the results of an earlier study on Asians in general, this study finds that the attachment to ethnic group culture may not necessarily depress the likelihood of integration into the U.S. political system (Lien 1994). This is additional evidence that pluralism, rather than assimilation, characterizes the American political culture. And in contrast to previous conceptions of ethnicity (Hurh and Kim 1984; Kim 1981), affiliation with a Korean American Protestant church does not have any independent influence on naturalization and voter registration. In the LAT survey of Koreans conducted on the eve of the Los Angeles Riots of 1992, we also learn that some factors that are hypothesized to shape ethnic group identity, such as the perception of group deprivation and experience of personal discrimination, may not be significant in predicting political integration for this group of recent arrivals. Conversely, in a later survey (of Asians in Southern California), discriminatory experience is found to be related to increased participation in activities other than voting and perceived deprivation is found to correlate with the rate of voting among citizens. This underscores the centrality of the socio-political context in shaping the character and impact of ethnicity on political participation.[1]

Taken as a whole, the significant and the null findings both reflect the fluidity of the roles of ethnic group identity, socioeconomic status, and demographic background in shaping Asian American political participation. A different model of political participation may be construed, depending on the state of the mobilization environment, the scope of the conception of ethnicity, and the form of participatory activities. This revelation fits well with V.O. Key's observation that "[t]he voice of the people is but an echo" (1966, 2). Political attitudes solicited through public opinion surveys therefore "constitute a *reaction* to political stimuli of a structural nature" (Cavanagh 1991, 96, emphasis original). And political participation is partly the product of the strategic mobilization by political parties, interest groups, and government elites (Rosenstone and Hansen 1993).

Because of the primary importance of political context in determining the impact of individual resources on political participation, the remaining space of this chapter offers a preliminary examination of the roles that some mobilization agents have played in affecting the shape of Asian American political participation over time.[2] These are, specifically, political parties, ethnic community organizations, and ethnic media. These are institutions that make links between individuals and the polity. For persons with recent immigration history, they are also agents of (re)socialization. It is hoped that the discussion will unfold some problems and prospects for the future of Asian American electoral participation.

Political parties

In the pluralistic American democracy, political parties and immigrant groups both have good reasons to become cordial bedfellows. As institutions aiming to win elections, political parties need immigrants to expand the electoral base, particularly where competition is high. As the principal agency of interest aggregation (Pomper 1980), parties are ideal institutions for protecting and advancing the interests of minority groups (Middleton 1991). Historically, immigrant groups identified and relied upon parties as their gateway to the American political process (Levy and Kramer 1973). During the late 19th and early 20th century, party organizations in many large cities of the East and Midwest were eager to exchange services for votes. In fact, many political jurisdictions allowed ¬non-citizens to vote prior to the 1920s when naturalization and voter registration were both under state jurisdiction. Thus, parties were powerful institutional forces for the political incorporation of immigrants.

Yet, recruiting new, and specifically Asian, immigrant voters and candidates has not been a major activity of contemporary party organizations. It is even less so in California. The main reason for this is that the resources of political parties have been severely reduced by the many statewide changes in electoral rules in the aftermath of the successful Progressive campaign to eradicate corruption and fraud (Lawson 1980; Schmidt 1992). This has resulted in party organizations that are highly regulated and severely underfunded. A related reason is that the political inclinations of Asians tend to be more independent and divided between the ideology of the left and the right. Further aggravating the situation is the fact that vast sums of money are usually required to prepare and distribute specialized mailers written in the various major Asian languages and to gain access to the pluralistic ethnic media market. Because of the above reasons, parties have not shown much enthusiasm in investing their limited resources on recruiting Asians.

The lack of attachment of Asians to either one of the major political parties, however, may be related partly to the indifference or naked antagonism displayed by both parties in the earlier part of California's history (Sandmeyer 1939; Saxton 1971). Even though this situation appears to have changed beginning with Jimmy Carter's 1976 campaign to cultivate Asian support, it is probably fair to say that both parties have been more interested in getting money from than developing votes in the Asian American community. Unfortunately, the fallout from the political fund-raising controversy of the 1996 election illustrates clearly that no matter how aggressively Asians may respond to major party strategies, their reliance on giving money as the avenue for gaining access and influence may actually do more harm than good to the political empowerment of the community.

It would be erroneous, however, to dismiss the positive influence of political parties on Asian participation. At the individual level, a stronger affiliation with major parties may indicate a greater likelihood to vote (Uhlaner 1991; Lien 1994). As an institution, political parties may provide a means of transition for those in the radical left to switch their participation strategies from protests to electoral politics. By the early 1970s, Wang (1991) notes that Asian American activists began to promote ethnic group concerns through local partisan organizations such as the Chinese American Democratic and Republican Clubs in San Francisco. Over time, they have also participated in party politics through ethnic-based organizations such as the Japanese American Democratic Club, the Nisei Voters League, the Korean American Political Association, the Filipino American Democratic Club, the Vietnamese American Democratic Club, and the Asian American Republican Association. Nevertheless, lack of proper funding, manpower, and stable organizational support from the state and/or national parties often limits the effectiveness of these local groups.

Ethnic community organizations

Like political parties, ethnic political organizations have a strong desire to articulate interests and/or to recruit members and to socialize or mobilize them for political action. Depending on the major function and nature of the organizations, membership in or identification with an ethnic organization may signify support for collective action against economic, political, and cultural discrimination. Or, it may suggest support for the preservation of ethnic culture and traditional values. In some cases, it may indicate the development of common political interests out of a concern over shared professional interests. In other cases, it may signify solidarity with the homeland political machine or ruling ideology. The disparate missions attached to these organizations certainly reflect their diverse organizational origins, which may be based on homeland district, religion, dialect, occupation, family lineage, ethnicity, panethnicity, social issues, and political principles or beliefs. However, these variegated organizations often overlap in clientele or membership and service or primary goal.

In contrast to political parties, ethnic organizations do not appear to be in decline. Instead, observers note a sharp rise in the number of ethnic-specific and panethnic organizations since the 1960s. Many have played a pivotal role in the development of the Asian American Movement by organizing protests and demonstrations to educate the public about anti-Asian racism, by arguing for Ethnic Studies programs, and by providing social services to the downtown communities (Wei 1993). Dominated by middle-class, U.S.-born, college-educated students or social service professionals, these progressive organizations were able to disrupt the community power structure and group boundaries coordinated by traditional organizations such as the Chinese Consolidated Benevolent Association (Wong 1982; Kwong 1987). Although their presence has increased the amount of internal division and strife within the organizational structure of the Asian American community, the dependency on outside funding—which rewards panethnic unity—also encourages the consolidation of diverse ethnic group interests and promotes the development of a pan-Asian based group consciousness (Espiritu 1992).

Given the low visibility and high diversity of Asians in U.S. society, established panethnic community organizations are often sought out by outsiders and relied upon by insiders to voice concerns for the growing community. A few examples of these organizations include the National Asian Pacific American Legal Consortium, Japanese American Citizens League, Organization of Chinese Americans, and Asian American Labor Alliance. Although some organizations readily admit that they are only advocating the pro-liberal agenda, they are nevertheless the ones that have been called upon by mainstream reporters, to testify in front of Congress, and to form coalitions or negotiate with non-Asian groups.

Following the end of the Civil Rights Era when the external environment called for change to survive, many progressive community organizations shifted their ideologies, strategies, and goals from radicalism to reform, from anti-war activism to lobbying and networking, from protests to elections, and from raising consciousness to engaging in leadership training (Nakanishi 1986a; Wei 1993). Due to the apparent weakness of the political parties, ethnic organizations have been encouraged to participate more in the political process by working independently of or together with partisan organizations to monitor legislative action, issue community concerns, organize grassroot campaigns, recruit political candidates, raise campaign funds, help draw legislative districts, register voters, and get out the vote. However, their influence can be negated by the criticisms over lack of political representation as well as by common organizational problems such as instability of economic resources, membership, personnel, and internal as well as inter-organizational conflicts over strategies, goals, and benefits.

Ethnic media

Similar to ethnic community organizations, ethnic media are brokers that serve the dual roles of ethnic maintenance and acculturation of new immigrants (Riggins 1992). The socialization role of the media is well documented in the literature (Chaffee and Yang 1990). For instance, to a group of Korean immigrants in California, exposure to U.S. and Korean media are the most consistent predictors of both political knowledge and discussions, outstripping formal education and social contacts (Chaffee, Nass, and Yang 1990). To the foreign-born generation, non-English language ethnic media are often their only source of homeland and U.S. news. They rely on these in-language media to maintain contacts with homeland cultures and developments. However, because many of the publications or programs are sponsored by foreign governments, exposure to these media may also influence immigrants' political loyalty to the homeland regimes (Kim 1981; Kwong 1987). Nevertheless, throughout history, Asians on the political left have used the ethnic media as a means of communication to organize support for homeland independence and democratization movements.

Increasingly, to the native-born or English-proficient Asians, English language ethnic media are the sources of ethnic attachment and ethnicization. According to Espiritu (1992), many ethnic media were responsible for identity and community building in the Asian American

Movement of the late 1960s and early 1970s. She notes that while the traditional ethnic press still held power, many pan-Asian periodicals such as *Gidra* and *Amerasia Journal* were founded by college students in the name of self-empowerment to address the overlooked issues of civil rights and racism. Over time, this concern for racial equality and justice propagated by the ethnic media has become part of the success stories of community redress movements. Also, some ethnic language publications have gradually broadened their scope to address the civil rights concerns of the ethnic-specific and pan-Asian communities. Because of their capacity to simultaneously maintain ethnic attachment, promote acculturation, and raise group consciousness, ethnic media are expected to continue playing a central and bridging role in mobilizing the political participation of Asian Americans.

In sum, an evaluation of these three mobilization agents suggests that beneath the relative passivity displayed in electoral politics, there is an undercurrent of political activism evident in the thriving organizational life of the Asian American community. This is so despite neglect by mainstream institutions and interference from homeland governments. Panethnic community-initiated reactions to recent events such as anti-Asian violence, biased college admission policies, English-only initiatives, discriminatory immigration legislation, and Asian-targeted political fund-raising investigations also suggest that it is possible to conceive a pan-Asian identity that transcends internal divisions over class, ethnicity, race, sex, religion, language, generation, and national origin. In the long run, these ethnic community and media organizations may provide the best hopes for translating the rich socioeconomic resources accumulated by Asians either before or after coming to the States into political assets.

NOTES

1. The differential impact of discriminatory experiences on different types of political participation in the two surveys may also accentuate the necessity to investigate in the future the meanings of various participatory forms for different population segments of Asians.

2. By recognizing the primacy of the environment, this study does not take the position that individual behavior can only be influenced by changes in the environment. Rather, the direction of influence can go both ways.

Voting and Registration in the Elections of 1992 and 1994

	Asian[a]	Latino[b]	Black	White[c]
November 1992 Election				
N (x1000)	5,129	14,688	21,039	157,837
CITIZENSHIP	55%	60%	95%	95%
REGISTRATION	31(57)[d]	35(59)	64	70
among College Grad.+	39(69)	60(82)	81	88
among Age 45+	40(65)	46(69)	73	78
VOTING	27(50)	29(48)	54	64
among College Grad.+	36(63)	56(77)	77	84
among Age 45+	37(59)	40(59)	65	72
November 1994 Election				
N (x1000)	4,849	17,476	21,799	160,317
CITIZENSHIP	55%	59%	96%	94%
REGISTRATION	29(52)	31(53)	59(61)	65(68)
among College Grad.+	34(59)	55(74)	72(77)	80(83)
among Age 45+	39(63)	44(66)	71(73)	75(78)
VOTING	22(39)	20(34)	37(39)	47(50)
among College Grad.+	27(47)	43(58)	57(61)	66(69)
among Age 45+	32(52)	32(47)	52(53)	60(62)

Appendix A--continued

Source: U.S. Bureau of Census. Data for the 1992 election are compiled from Current Population Reports, Series P-20, No. 466. Data for the 1994 election are retrieved from electronic data files released by the Census Bureau in July 1996.

[a]Asian or Pacific Islanders. All populations referred to in this table are those of age 18 or over.

[b]Hispanic-origin persons. They can be of any race. According to results of the March 1992 CPS, about 95.2% of Hispanic-origin persons are of white race.

[c]Some whites may be of Hispanic origin. Results of March 1992 CPS indicate that about one tenth of whites are of Hispanic origin.

[d]Percentages in parenthesis are those among citizens.

A Comparison of Selected Characteristics of Asian Americans from Four Sources

SOURCE	(1) 1984 Sample[a]	(2) 1993 Sample	(3) 1990 Census	(4) 1992 CPS
COVERAGE	California	6 counties S. California	Los Angeles County, CA	Nation
Asian N=	308	221	929[b]	5,129[b]
% Asian	19	18	11	3
% Citizenship	65	70	56	55
% Foreign-born	57	52	70	
% College Degree or more (among those age 25+)				
	39	47	38	35
% Family Income (50K or more)				
	27[c]	39	38	30
%Male	60	52	49	47
% Age 45+	25	22	36	
% Chinese	22	25	27	
% Japanese	23	21	14	
% Korean	29	10	15	
% Filipino	16	18	24	
% Vietnamese	4	13	7	
% Registration	55(77)[d]	47(68)	31(57)	
% Voting	48(69)	37(53)	27(50)	

Appendix B-continued
[a] Information on the 1984 sample is taken from a 1984 California Ethnicity Survey Conducted by Bruce Cain and others and made available to the author through the University of California Institute of Social Science Research.
[b] Numbers are in thousands. The Los Angeles County figures are for Asians only, Pacific Islanders are excluded from the analysis. Unlike most of the figures for columns 1, 2, and 4, which were calculated among those age 18 and over, most of the figures for LA County were calculated among the entire population.
[c] Those with a family income of 40K or more.
[d] Figures in parentheses are those among citizens.

A Comparison of Selected Characteristics of Korean Americans in Los Angeles County to the 1990 Census

	1992 Sample	1990 Census
% Citizenship	36	45
% Foreign-born	99	82
% College Degree or more (among those age 25+)		
	49	34
% Family Income (50K or more)		
	31	29
% Female	51	46[a]
% Registration	18(51)[b]	

[a] This percentage is calculated among those age 16 and over.
[b] The percentage in parenthesis is that among citizens.

Question Wording for the Surveys of Southern Californians and of Koreans in Los Angeles
(S=in Southern California survey, K=in Koreans in Los Angeles survey, SK=in both Southern California and Koreans in LA surveys)

I. POLITICAL PARTICIPATION

SK. *Registration* (asked of respondents who are citizens) "Some people are registered to vote and other people are not. Do you know for sure if your name is presently recorded in the voter registration book of the Election District where you now live? [IF YES] Are you registered in a political party, or have you declined to be registered in any specific party—that is to say, are you an Independent? [IF REGISTERED IN A PARTY] Which party is that?"

S. *Voting* (asked of those who are registered to vote) "Sometimes it happens that people don't get to vote in every single election. Did you vote for President this past November, or did something prevent you from voting, or did you choose not to vote? (IF VOTED) Who did you vote for: Bill Clinton, the Democrat, or George Bush, the Republican, or Ross Perot, the Independent, or did you vote for someone else?"

S. *Participation Other than Voting* (asked of everyone) "Some people participate in politics and some people do not. During the past four years, have you participated in any type of political activity in your community? For example, have you written or phoned a government official, or donated money to a political campaign, or attended a political function or volunteered for a political cause or have you done something else or don't you participate in politics?" (Accept up to four replies)

SK. *Citizenship* "Are you a citizen of the United States, or not?"

K. *Citizenship Intent* (asked of noncitizens) "Do you expect to become a citizen of the United States in the next few years, or not?"

II. SOCIODEMOGRAPHIC BACKGROUND

SK. *Education* "What is the highest grade of regular school or college that you finished and got credit for? (IF HIGH SCHOOL GRADUATE) After graduating from high school, did you complete some technical training like secretarial school, art school, or trade school, or something like that?"

K. *Place of Education* "Were you educated mainly in Korea, mainly in the United States or were you educated in both places?"

SK. *Family Income* "If you added together the yearly incomes of all the members of your family living at home last year, would the total of all their incomes be less than $20,000 . . . or more than $40,000 . . . or somewhere in between? (IF LESS THAN $20,000) Would the total of all their incomes be less than $10,000? (IF IN-BETWEEN) Would the total of all their incomes be less than $30,000 or more than $30,000? (IF MORE THAN $40,000) Would the total of all their incomes be between $40,000 and $50,000 . . . or between $50,000 and $60,000 . . . or more than that?"

SK. *Employment* "What were you doing most of last week: working full-time, or working part-time, or were you self-employed, or keeping house, or going to school, or are you looking for work, or retired, or what? (IF ILL, ON VACATION, OR ON STRIKE, RECORD AS 'WORKING.' IF LOOKING FOR WORK, ASK) Have you looked for a full- or a part-time job in the past four weeks?" (IF YES, RECORD AS 'LOOKING FOR WORK.' IF NO, RECORD AS 'NOT LOOKING FOR WORK.')

SK. *Age* "How old were you on your last birthday?

S. *Age Group* Well, does your age fall between 18-21, or 22- 24, or 25-39, or 40-44, or 45-64, are you older than that?"

S. *Length of Stay* "Have you lived all your life in Southern California, or not? (IF NO) Well, how long have you lived in Southern California?"

K. _____ "How many years have you lived in the United States on a permanent basis?"

S. *Immigration Generation* "Were you born outside of the United States or not? (IF NO) Were either or both of your parents born outside of the United States, or not?"

K. *Immigration Generation/Nationality* "In what country were you born? (IF BORN IN THE UNITED STATES, ASK) Were you born in California or in some other part of the United States?"

S. *Race/Ethnicity* "What is your race: Is it white, or black, or Asian, or do you consider yourself of some other race?" and "Are you, yourself, of Latino or Hispanic descent—for example Mexican, or Puerto Rican, or Cuban, or some other Spanish background—or are you not?"

S. *Asian Country of Origin* "What country in Asia are you or your ancestors from?"

III. SOCIO-PSYCHOLOGICAL FACTORS

A. Group Consciousness

S. *Own Group Most Deprived* "Which group, if any, do you think suffers the most discrimination in your community these days? Is there another group which you feel suffers almost as much discrimination?"

S. *Group Condition Bad* "How about [one of the four ethnic groups] in Southern California and their ability to get adequate housing, and education, and job opportunities and things like that? Generally speaking, do you think conditions for [same ethnic group as mentioned above] in Southern California are very good, or good, or bad, or very bad?"

K. *Relative Group Condition* "How would you rate the situation for Koreans relative to other minorities in Southern California such as blacks and Latinos: do you think Koreans are generally better off, or are they worse off or are they in just about the same situation as other minorities?"

S. *Racial Discrimination a Problem* "How big a problem is racial discrimination in your community? Is it a major problem, a moderate-sized problem, a minor problem or not a problem at all?"

K. *Primary Barrier for Group* "What do you think is the primary thing holding Koreans back in Southern California: is it racism and discrimination, or the language barrier, or lack of interest in getting involved in mainstream society, or cultural differences or lack of adequate job training or something else?

S. *Personal Experience of Discrimination* "During the time you've lived in Southern California, have you personally been discriminated against a great deal, a fair amount, some but not much, or not at all?"

K. _____ "Because you are Korean, have you personally been discriminated against a great deal, a fair amount, some but not much, or practically not at all during the time you've lived in Southern California?"

SK. *Ways Discriminated* (asked of those being discriminated against) "In which of these ways, if any, have you experienced discrimination during the time you've lived in Southern California: in jobs or promotion, in education, in housing, in dealing with a government agency, in dealing with a business or retail establishment, from your neighbors, from strangers in a public place or in some other way? Is there another way you've experienced discrimination?"

S. *Victim of Hate Crime* "Have you ever been the victim of a 'hate crime' in Southern California, that is, have you had someone verbally or physically abuse you, or damage your property, specifically because you belong to a certain race or ethnic group?"

K._____ "In the past few years, have you ever been verbally or physically abused by a non-Korean, or not? (IF YES, ASK:) Were racial differences a reason for any of those conflicts, or was race not a factor in any of those conflicts?"

S. *Hear Racial Slurs about Asians* "How often would you say you hear racial slurs about Asians made by the people you come in contact with? Do you hear them very often, fairly often, fairly infrequently or very infrequently?"

S. *Know of Asian American Leaders* "Right now, who do you think is the most prominent American of Asian background?"

S. *Know of Asian American History* "To the best of your knowledge, when did the first Asians settle in California: about 25 years ago or about 50 years ago or about 100 years ago?"

S. *Know of Internment of Japanese Americans* "To the best of your knowledge, during World War II, did the U.S. government gather up American citizens of Japanese descent and place them in internment camps because of fear they were security risks, or not?"

S. *Support Reparations* "The United States government has recently awarded reparation payments to the Japanese-Americans whom it did confine in internment camps during World War II. Do you favor or oppose the idea of awarding reparations to those people? (IF FAVOR OR OPPOSE) Do you (favor/oppose) that strongly or (favor/oppose) that somewhat?

S. *(Dis)satisfaction with Life* "All things considered, would you say you are satisfied or dissatisfied these days with the community in which you live? Are you entirely (satisfied/dissatisfied), or mostly (satisfied/dissatisfied), or are you somewhat (satisfied/dissatisfied) these days with the community in which you live?

B. Acculturation/Integration

S. *Crossracial Friendship* "Thinking for a moment of blacks, whites, Latinos and Asians, do you yourself know any person of another race whom you consider a close personal friend or not?"

K. _____ "Are any of your friends white, or black, or Latino or non-Korean Asian or what?"

SK. *Interracial Marriage* "Would you approve or disapprove if someone in your family married a person of a different racial or ethnic background than yours—or wouldn't you care about that one way or the other? (IF APPROVE OR DISAPPROVE) Do you (approve/disapprove) strongly or (approve/disapprove) somewhat?"

K. *English Fluency* "How well do you speak English: very well, or just well, or not well, or not at all?"

K. *Speaking with Whites* "In an average week, how many white people do you talk to: over twenty-five, between ten and twenty-five, between five and ten, between one and five or don't you talk to any white people in an average week?"

K. *Religious Affiliation* "Are you currently a member of a particular religious parish or congregation that has your name on its registers or that you support with contributions, or not?"

K. *Language Use* "In your everyday life, do you speak Korean exclusively, mostly Korean, Korean and English equally, mostly English or do you speak English exclusively?"

K. *Media Use* "Are the periodicals you read and the broadcasts you listen to exclusively Korean, mostly Korean, about half-Korean and half English or mostly English or mostly English or English exclusively?"

K. *Business Contacts* "Are your business and financial transactions conducted exclusively with Koreans, mostly with Koreans, about half with Korean and half with non-Koreans, with mostly non-Koreans or with non-Koreans exclusively?"

C. Attachment to Ethnic Culture

K. *Preserve Korean Culture* "How important is it to preserve Korean culture for future generations of Koreans in America? Is it very important, or fairly important, or not very important, or hardly important at all?"

K. *Expect to Return to Korea* "Generally speaking, where do you expect you and your children will end up living in the years to come: in

Korea, in California, somewhere in the United States other than California or elsewhere?"

K. *Koreans in Neighborhood* "How would you describe the racial and ethnic makeup of the neighborhood where you live? Would you say it is mostly white, or mostly black, or mostly Latino, or mostly Korean, or is it mostly non-Korean Asian, or is it mostly some other ethnic/racial group, or would you say the racial and/or ethnic makeup is pretty evenly mixed?"

K. *Importance of Koreatown* "How important is Koreatown in Los Angeles to you personally as a business, cultural and social center: is it the most important place to you, one of many important places, not as important as other places or not important to you at all?"

IV. POLICY PREFERENCES AND OTHER POLITICAL ORIENTATIONS

S. *College Admission* "As you may know, Asians make up about 10 percent of California's population but they comprise about 28 percent of the students in the University of California system. Which of these statements comes closer to your view about that: 'If Asians are better qualified, more of them should be admitted to college than others.' or 'Despite qualifications, the racial makeup in colleges should generally mirror the population as a whole.'"

S. *Ban Immigration* "Some people have proposed that all LEGAL foreign immigration to the U.S. be stopped for a period of 3 years. Do you favor or oppose that proposal? (IF FAVOR OR OPPOSE) Do you (favor/oppose) that strongly or (favor/oppose) that somewhat?"

S. *Asylum Hearing* "As you may know, several hundred Chinese nationals recently attempted to land their boats in California in order to seek asylum in this country. The U.S. Coast Guard and Mexico intercepted the boats before they entered American waters and the Chinese were returned to their homeland without their cases being heard by the U.S. government. Do you approve of the decision to send the Chinese boat people back to their homeland without hearings or do you think the United States should have agreed to hear each person's case for asylum? (IF APPROVE OR FEEL EACH SHOULD HAVE GOTTEN HEARING) Do you feel strongly or not strongly about that?"

S. *Support Reparations* "The United States government has recently awarded reparation payments to the Japanese-Americans whom it did confine in internment camps during World War II. Do you favor or oppose the idea of awarding reparations to those people? (IF FAVOR OR OPPOSE) Do you (favor/oppose) that strongly or (favor/oppose) that somewhat?

S. *Political Ideology* "How would you describe your views on most matters having to do with politics? Do you generally think of yourself as very liberal, or somewhat liberal, or middle-of-the-road, or somewhat conservative, or very conservative?

S. *Perceived Vote for Asian Candidates* "How do you think most people you know would feel about voting for an Asian-American for political office? Do you think they would be favorably disposed to that, or would that make them uncomfortable, or would that not make a difference to them one way or the other?

The Korean American Perspective on Inter-Group Relations in Los Angeles, February-March 1992

Q. "Overall, how would you rate relations between Koreans and other races and ethnic groups in Southern California these days: excellent, good, not so good or poor?"

Excellent	4%
Good	31%
Not Good	58%

Q. "Do you think race relations between Koreans and other groups living in Southern California are getting better, getting worse or staying about the same?"

Better	39%
Worse	19%
Same	34%
Not Sure	8%

Q. "Who or what do you think is primarily responsible for the conflicts which have been occurring between blacks and Koreans?"

Blacks	16%
Koreans	15%
Both	53%

Q. "Do you think the news media have exaggerated the amount of conflict between Koreans and blacks in Southern California, or have they underplayed the amount of conflict or have the media given that conflict the right amount of attention?"

Exaggerated	78%
Underplayed	5%
Right Amount	18%

Q. "What's the most important problem facing Southern California today? Is there another problem that is almost as urgent?" (ACCEPTED UP TO TWO REPLIES)

Recession	38%
Crime	37%
Racism/Racial Tensions	18%
Drugs	13%

Q. "All things considered, would you say you are satisfied or dissatisfied with the way your life is going these days? Are you entirely (satisfied/dissatisfied) or mostly (satisfied/ dissatisfied) or are you somewhat (satisfied/dissatisfied) with the way your life is going these days?"

Satisfied	74%
Neutral	15%
Dissatisfied	9%

Q. "How do you think most blacks/Latinos you come in contact with feel about you? Do you think most of them like you, or dislike you, or do you think most of them neither like nor dislike you?"

	Black	Latino
No Contact	16%	10%
Like	34%	47%
Dislike	49%	5%
Neither	32%	28%
Nor Sure	9%	10%

Q. "Generally speaking, do you think Koreans feel least favorably toward whites, blacks or Latinos or non-Korean Asians or toward no group in particular?"

No Group	18%
White	9%
Black	64%
Lationo	8%
Non-Korean Asian	1%

Q. "In an average week, how many (black/Latino) people do you talk to: over twenty-five, between ten and twenty-five, between five and ten, between one and five or don't you talk to any black people in an average week?"

	Black	Latino
Over 25	14%	20%
10-25	6%	10%
5-10	11%	14%
1-5	30%	31%
None	40%	25%

Q. "Are any of your friends white, or black, or Latino, or non-Korean Asians or what?"

None	36%
White	50%
Black	2%
Latino	5%
Non-Korean Asian	7%

References

Abramson, Paul R., and William Claggett. (1991). Racial differences in self-reported and validated turnout in the 1988 presidential election. *Journal of Politics* 53:186-197.

Abramson, Paul R., and William Claggett. (1992). The quality of record keeping and racial differences in validated turnout. *Journal of Politics* 54:871-880.

Aguilar-San Juan, Karin. (Ed.). (1994). *The State of Asia America: Activism and Resistance in the 1990s*. Boston, MA: South End Press.

Almaguer, Tomas. (1994). *Racial Fault Lines: The Historical Origins of White Supremacy in California*. Berkeley: University of California Press.

Ancheta, Angelo N., and Kathryn K. Imahara. (1993). Multi-ethnic voting rights: Redefining vote dilution in communities of color. *University of San Francisco Law Review* 27:815-872.

Babbie, Earl. (1989). *The Practice of Social Research, 5th Ed*. Belmont, CA: Wadsworth Publishing Company.

Bai, Su Sun. (1991). Affirmative pursuit of political equality for Asian Pacific Americans: Reclaiming the Voting Rights Act. *University of Pennsylvania Law Review* 139:731-767.

Barkan, Elliott R. (1983). Whom shall we integrate: A comparative analysis of the immigration and naturalization trends of Asians before and after the 1965 Immigration Act (1951-1978). *Journal of American Ethnic History* 3:29-55.

Barth, Fredrick. (1969). *Ethnic Groups and Boundaries*. Boston: Little Brown.

Baxter, Sandra, and Marjorie Lansing. (1983). *Women and Politics: The Visible Minority*. Ann Arbor: University of Michigan Press.

Bennett, Claudette. (1992). *The Asian and Pacific Islander Population in the United States*. Washington, D.C.: U.S. Department of Commerce, Bureau of the Census.

Bennett, Stephen, and David Resnick. (1990). The implications of nonvoting for democracy in the United States. *American Journal of Political Science* 34:771-802.

Berelson, Bernard R., Paul F. Lazarsfeld, and William N. McPhee. (1954). *Voting*. Chicago: University of Chicago Press.

Black, Jerome, Richard Niemi, and Gilbert B. Powell, Jr. (1987). Age, resistance, and political learning in a new environment: The case of Canadian immigrants. *Comparative Politics* 20:73-84.

Bobo, Lawrence, and Franklin D. Gilliam, Jr. (1990). Race, sociopolitical participation, and black empowerment. *American Political Science Review* 84:377-393.

Button, James. (1989). *Blacks and Social Change*. Princeton, NJ: Princeton University Press.

Cain, Bruce, and Roderick Kiewiet. (1986). "Minorities in California." Proceedings from a public symposium, 5 March, Pasadena, California.

Caldeira, Gregory A., Samuel C. Patterson, and Gregory A. Markko. (1985). The mobilization of voters in congressional elections. *Journal of Politics* 47:490-509.

Calderon, Jose Zapata. (1991). "Mexican American Politics in a Multi-ethnic Community: The Case of Monterey Park: 1985-1990." Ph.D. Dissertation, University of California, Los Angeles.

Calvert, Jerry W., and Jack Gilchrist. (1993). Do the rules count? Election law reform and voter turnout in the 1988 election. Paper delivered at the Annual Meeting of the American Political Science Association, Washington, D.C.

Calvo, Maria A., and Steven J. Rosenstone. (1989). *Hispanic Political Participation*. San Antonio: Southwest Voter Research Institute.

Campbell, Angus, Philip E. Converse, Warren E. Miller, and Donald E. Stokes. (1960). *The American Voter*. New York: John Wiley and Sons.

Cavanagh, Thomas E. (1991). When turnout matters: Mobilization and conversion as determinants of election outcomes. In William Crotty (ed.), *Political Participation and American Democracy*, pp. 89-112. Westport, CT: Greenwood Press.

Cha, Marn J. (1977). An ethnic political orientation as a function of assimilation: With reference to Koreans in Los Angeles. In Hyung-chan Kim, (ed.), *The Korean Diaspora*. Santa Barbara, CA: ABC-Clio.

Chaffee, Steven H., Clifford I. Nass, and Seung-Mock Yang. (1990). The bridging role of television in immigrant political socialization. *Human Communication Research* 17:266-288.

Chaffee, Steven H., and Seung-Mock Yang. (1990). Communication and political socialization. In O. Ichilov (ed.), *Political Socialization, Citizenship, Education, and Democracy*, pp. 137-157. New York: Teachers College Press.

Chan, Sucheng. (1991). *Asian Americans: An Interpretive History*. Boston: Twayne.

Chang, Edward. (1988). Korean community politics in Los Angeles: The impact of Kwangju Uprising. *Amerasia* 14(1):51-67.

Chang, Edward. (1994). America's first multiethnic 'riots'. In Karin Aguilar-San Juan, (ed.), *The State of Asian America*, pp. 101-117. Boston, MA: South End Press.

Cheng Lucie, and Edna Bonacich. (1984). *Labor Immigration under Capitalism: Asian Workers in the United States before World War II.* Berkeley: University of California Press.

Chow, Esther Ngan-Ling. (1987). The development of feminist consciousness among Asian American women. *Gender and Society* 1:284-299.

Citrin, Jack. (1977). Political alienation as a social indicator: Attitudes and action. *Social Indicator Research* 4:381-419.

Commission on Wartime Relocation and Internment of Civilians. (1982). *Personal Justice Denied.* Washington, DC: The Commission on Wartime Relocation and Internment of Civilians.

Converse, Philip E. (1969). Of time and partisan stability. *Comparative Political Studies* 2:139-177.

Conway, M. Margaret. (1991a). *Political Participation in the United States*, 2nd Ed. Washington, D.C.: Congressional Quarterly.

Conway, M. Margaret. (1991b). The study of political participation: Past, present, and future. In William Crotty (ed.), *Political Science: Vol. III*, pp. 31-49. Evanston, IL: Northwestern University Press.

Cox, Gary W., and Michael C. Munger. (1989). Closeness, expenditures, and turnout in the 1982 U.S. House elections. *American Political Science Review* 83:217-231.

Dahl, Robert A. (1961). *Who Governs? Democracy and Power in an American City.* New Haven, CT: Yale University Press.

Daniels, Roger. (1962). *The Politics of Prejudice: The Anti-Japanese Movement in California and the Struggle for Japanese Exclusion.* Berkeley: University of California Press.

Daniels, Roger. (1988). *Asian America: Chinese and Japanese in the United States Since 1850.* Seattle: University of Washington Press.

Daniels, Roger. (1990). *Coming to America.* New York: HarperCollins.

Dawson, Michael. (1994). *Behind the Mule: Race and Class in African-American Politics.* Princeton, NJ: Princeton University Press.

de la Garza, Rodolfo O. (Ed.). (1987). *Ignored Voices.* Austin, TX: University of Texas Press.

de la Garza, Rodolfo O., and Louis DeSipio. (Eds.). (1992). *From Rhetoric to Reality: Latino Politics in the 1988 Elections.* Boulder, CO: Westview Press.

de la Garza, Rodolfo O., and Louis DeSipio. (Eds.). (1996). *Ethnic Ironies: Latino Politics in the 1992 Elections.* Boulder, CO: Westview Press.

de la Garza, Rodolfo O., Louis DeSipio, F. Chris Garcia, John A. Garcia, and Angelo Falcon. (1992). *Latino Voices: Mexican, Puerto Rican, and Cuban Perspectives on American Politics.* Boulder, CO: Westview Press.

Denigelis, Nicholas L. (1978). Black political participation in the United States: Some recent evidence. *American Sociological Review* 43:756-771.

Dennis, Jack. (1991). The study of electoral behavior. In William Crotty (ed.), *Political Science: Vol. III*, pp. 51-89. Evanston, IL: Northwestern University Press.

DeSipio, Louis. (1996). *Counting on the Latino Vote: Latinos as a New Electorate.* Charlottesville, VA: University Press of Virginia.

Din, Grant. (1984). "An Analysis of Asian/Pacific Registration and Voting Patterns in San Francisco." Master's thesis, Claremont Graduate School.

Efron, Sonni. (1990, August 16). Politics are changing for Asian-Americans. *Los Angeles Times,* A1, A43-A44.

Ellison, Christopher G., and David A. Gay. (1989). Black political participation revisited: A test of compensatory, ethnic community, and public arena models. *Social Science Quarterly* 70:101-19.

Erie, Steven P., and Harold Brackman. (1993). "Paths to Political Incorporation for Latinos and Asian Pacifics in California." University of California: The California Policy Seminar.

Espina, Marina E. (1988). *Filipinos in Louisiana.* New Orleans: A.F. Laborde & Sons.

Espiritu, Yen L. (1992). *Asian American Panethnicity.* Philadelphia: Temple University Press.

Espiritu, Yen L., and Paul Ong. (1994). Class constraints on racial solidarity among Asian Americans. In Paul Ong, Edna Bonacich, and Lucie Cheng (eds.), *The New Asian Immigration in Los Angeles and Global Restructuring,* pp. 295-321. Philadelphia: Temple University Press.

Feagin, Joe, and Clairece Feagin. (1993). *Racial and Ethnic Relations, 4th Ed.* Englewood Cliffs, NJ: Prentice-Hall.

Field Institute. (1990, August). A digest on California's political demography. *California Opinion Index.*

Finifter, Ada W., and Bernard M. Finifter. (1989). Party identification and political adaptation of American migrants in Australia. *Journal of Politics* 51:599-630.

Fong, Timothy P. (1994). *The First Suburban Chinatown: The Remaking of Monterey Park, California.* Philadelphia: Temple University Press.

Freer, Regina. (1994). Black-Korean Conflict. In Mark Baldassare, ed., *The Los Angeles Riots: Lessons for the Urban Future.* Boulder: Westview.

Fuchs, Lawrence H. (1990). *The American Kaleidoscope: Race, Ethnicity, and the Civic Culture.* Hanover, CT: Wesleyan University Press.

Fugita, Stephen, and David O'Brien. (1991). *Japanese American Ethnicity: The Persistence of Community.* Seattle, WA: University of Washington Press.

Gant, Michael M., and William Lyons. (1992). Democratic theory, non-voting and public policy: The 1972-1988 Presidential elections. *American Politics Quarterly* 21:185-204.

Garcia, Alma. (1989). The development of Chicana feminist discourse, 1790-1980. *Gender and Society* 3:217-238.

Garcia, F. Chris, John Garcia, Rodolfo de la Garza, and Angelo Falcon. (1992). The effects of ethnic partisanship on electoral behavior. Paper delivered at the Annual Meeting of the American Political Science Association, Chicago.

Garcia, John A. (1987). The political integration of Mexican immigrants: Examining some political orientations. *International Migration Review* 21:372-389.

Ger, Yeong-Kuang. (1985). "Ethnic Identity and Ethnic Political Development: The Experience of Chinese Americans." Ph.D. Dissertation. University of Wisconsin.

Gitelman, Zvi. (1982). *Becoming Israelies: Political Socialization of Soviet and American Immigrants.* New York: Praeger.

Gordon, Milton M. (1964). *Assimilation in America Life.* New York: Oxford University Press.

Gordon, Milton M. (1978). *Human Nature, Class, and Ethnicity.* New York: Oxford University Press.

Hardy-Fanta, Carol. (1993). *Latina Politics, Latino Politics: Gender, Culture, and Political Participation in Boston.* Philadelphia: Temple University Press.

Harles, John. (1993). *Politics in the Lifeboat.* Boulder, CO: Westview.

Hatamiya, Leslie T. (1993). *Righting a Wrong: Japanese Americans and the Passage of the Civil Liberties Act of 1988.* Stanford, CA: Stanford University Press.

Hero, Rodney E. (1992). *Latinos and the U.S. Political System.* Philadelphia: Temple University Press.

Hing, Bill Ong. (1993). *Making and Remaking Asian America Through Immigration Policy 1850-1990.* Stanford, CA: Stanford University Press.

Horton, John. 1995. *The Politics of Diversity: Immigration, Resistance, and Change in Monterey Park, California.* Philadelphia: Temple University Press.

Hurh, Won M. (1980). Towards a Korean-American ethnicity: Some theoretical models. *Ethnic and Racial Studies* 3:444-464.

Hurh, Won M., and Kwang C. Kim. (1984a). *Korean Immigrants in America: A Structural Analysis of Ethnic Confinement and Adhesive Adaptation.* Madison, NJ: Farleigh Dickinson University Press.

Hurh, Won M., and Kwang C. Kim. (1984b). Adhesive sociocultural adaptation of Korean immigrants in the United States: An alternative strategy of minority adaptation. *International Migration Review* 18:188-217.

Hurh, Won M., and Kwang C. Kim. (1989). The 'success' image of Asian Americans: Its validity, and its practical and theoretical implications. *Ethnic and Racial Studies* 12:512-535.

Hutchison, Ray. (1988). The Hispanic community in Chicago: A study of population growth and acculturation. In Cora Marrett and Cheryl Leggon (eds.), *Research in Race and Ethnic Relations*, pp. 193-229. Greenwich, CT: JAI Press.

Hutnik, Nimmi. (1986). Patterns of ethnic minority identification and modes of social adaptation. *Ethnic and Racial Studies* 9:150-167.

Isajiw, Wsevolod W. (1974). Definitions of ethnicity. *Ethnicity* 1:111-124.

Jackson, Robert A. (1996). A reassessment of voter mobilization. *Political Research Quarterly* 49:331-349.

Jasso, Guillermina, and Mark R. Rosenzweig. (1990). *The New Chosen People: Immigrants in the United States.* New York: Russell Sage Foundation.

Jennings, Jerry T. (1993). *Voting and Registration in the Election of November 1992.* Washington, D.C.: U.S. Government Printing Office.

Jennings, M. Kent. (1989). The crystallization of orientations. In M. Kent Jennings et al., *Continuities in Political Action: A Longitudinal Study of Political Orientations in Three Western Democracies,* pp. 313-348. Berlin, Germany: Walter de Gruyter & Co.

Jensen, Richard J., and Cara J. Abeyta. (1987). The minority in the middle: Asian-American dissent in the 1960s and 1970s. *Western Journal of Speech Communication* 51:402-416.

Jo, Moon H. (1984). The putative political complacency of Asian Americans. *Political Psychology* 5:583-685.

Jo, Yung-hwan. (Ed.). (1980). *Political participation of Asian-Americans.* Chicago: Pacific/Asian American Mental Health Research Center.

Jo, Yung-Hwan. (1982). Problems and strategies of participation in American politics. In Eui-Young Yu, Earl Phillips, and Eun Sik Yang, (eds.), *Koreans in Los Angeles: Prospects and Promises,* pp. 203-218. Los Angeles: Koryo Research Institute.

Jun, Sun P. (1984). "Political Behavior of Blacks, Hispanics, and Asians in the United States." M.A. Thesis, Iowa State University.

Jung, Carolyn. (1993, August 5). 49-year wait ends for ex-internee. *San Jose Mercury News,* A15.

Keefe, Susan E., and Amado M. Padilla. (1987). *Chicano Ethnicity.* Albuquerque, NM: University of New Mexico Press.

Key, V.O., Jr. (1966). *The Responsible Electorate.* Cambridge, MA: Harvard University Press.

Keyes, Charles F. (1981). *Ethnic Change.* Seattle: University of Washington Press.

Kiecolt, K. Jill, and Laura E. Nathan, (1985). *Secondary Analysis of Survey Data.* Newbury Park, CA: Sage.

Kim, David, and Charles Wong. (1977). Business development in Koreatown, Los Angeles. In Hyung-chan Kim, (ed.), *The Korean Diaspora.* Santa Barbara, CA: ABC-Clio.

Kim, Hyung-chan. (Ed.). (1992). *Asian Americans and the Supreme Court: A Documentary History.* Westport, CT: Greenwood Press.

Kim, Hyung-chan. (1994). *A Legal History of Asian Americans, 1790-1990.* Westport, CT: Greenwood Press.

Kim, Hyung-chan. (Ed.). (1996). *Asian Americans and Congress: A Documentary History.* Westport, CT: Greenwood Press.

Kim, Illsoo. (1981). *New Urban Immigrants: The Korean Community in New York.* Princeton, NJ: Princeton University Press.

Kim, Kwang Chung, and Won Moo Hurh. (1993). Beyond assimilation and pluralism: Syncretic sociocultural adaptation of Korean Immigrants in the United States. *Ethnic and Racial Studies* 16:696-713.

Kim, Pan Suk, and Gregory B. Lewis. (1994). Asian Americans in the public service: Success, diversity, and discrimination. *Public Administration Review* 54: 285-290.

Kinder, Donald R., and David O. Sears. (1985). Public opinion and political action. In Gardner Lindzey and Elliot Aronson (eds.), *Handbook of Social Psychology, Vol. 2, 3rd Ed.* New York: Random House.

Kitano, Harry. (1976). *Japanese Americans: The Evolution of a Subculture.* Englewood Cliffs, NJ: Prentice-Hall.

Kitano, Harry L., and Roger Daniels. (1995). *Asian-Americans:Emerging Minorities, 2nd Ed.* Englewood Cliffs, NJ: Prentice-Hall.

Kwoh, Stewart, and Mindy Hui. (1993). Empowering our communities: Political policy. In *The State of Asian Pacific America: Policy Issues to the Year 2020*, pp. 189-198. Los Angeles: LEAP Asian Pacific American Public Policy Institute and UCLA Asian American Studies Center.

Kwong, Peter. (1987). *The New Chinatown.* New York: Hill and Wang.

Lai, James S. (1994). "At the Threshold of the Golden Door—Ethnic Politics and Pan-Asian Pacific American Coalition Building: A Case Study of the Special 1991 California 46th Assembly District Primary Election." M.A. Thesis, University of California at Los Angeles.

Lawson, Kay. (1980). California: The uncertainties of reform. In Gerald Pomper (ed.), *Party Renewal in America*, pp. 116-138. New York: Praeger.

Lee, Dong Ok. (1992). Commodification of ethnicity: The sociospatial reproduction of immigrant entrepreneurs. *Urban Affairs Quarterly* 28: 258-275.

Lee, Hwasoo. (1980). Toward Korean-American participation and representation in American politics: The case of Los Angeles. In Yung-hwan Jo (eds.), *Political Participation of Asian Americans*, pp. 74-89. Chicago: Pacific/ Asian American Mental Health Research Center.

Lee, Robert. (1996). The hidden world of Asian immigrant radicalism. In Paul Buhle and Dan Georgakas (eds.), *The Immigrant Left in the United States*, pp. 256-288. Albany, NY: State University of New York Press.

Lee, Sharon. (1989). Asian immigration and American race-relations: From exclusion to acceptance? *Ethnic and Racial Studies* 12:368-390.

Leighley, Jan. (1995). Attitudes, opportunies and incentives: A field essay on political participation. *Political Research Quarterly* 48:181-209.

Leighley, Jan, and Jonathan Nagler. (1992a). Socioeconomic class bias in turnout, 1964-1988: The voters remain the same. *American Political Science Review* 86:725-736.

Leighley, Jan, and Jonathan Nagler. (1992b). Individual and systemic influences on turnout: Who votes? 1984. *Journal of Politics* 54:718-740.

Leighley, Jan, and Arnold Vedlitz. (1994). Group identification and political behavior: Contrasts among African-Americans, Mexican-Americans and Asian-Americans. Paper presented at the Annual Meeting of the American Political Science Association, New York.

Leung, Vitus, and Don Mar. (1991). 1990 Census outreach to Asian and Pacific Americans in the San Francisco Metropolitan Area. *Asian American Policy Review* 2:3-15.

Levy, Mark R., and Michael S. Kramer. (1973). *The Ethnic Factor:How America's Minorities Decide Elections.* New York: Simon and Schuster.

Lew, Julie. (1987, August 27). Asian Americans more willingly stuff campaign war-chests than ballot boxes. *East/West*, 1.

Lien, Pei-te. (1992). Meanings of ethnicity in political participation: The case of Asian Americans. Paper presented at the Annual Meeting of the Southern Political Science Association, Atlanta, GA.

Lien, Pei-te. (1993). Ethnicity and political participation: A comparison between Asian and Mexican Americans. Paper presented at the Annual Meeting of the American Political Science Association, Washington, DC.

Lien, Pei-te. (1994). Ethnicity and political participation: A comparison between Asian and Mexican Americans. *Political Behavior* 16:237-264.

Lien, Pei-te. (1995). "The Political Participation of Asian Americans in the Early 1990s." Ph.D. Dissertation. University of Florida.

Light, Ivan, and Edna Bonacich. (1988). *Immigrant Entrepreneurs: Koreans in Los Angeles, 1965-1982.* Berkeley: University of California Press.

Lim, Gerard. (1995, September 1). Once burned, twice shy. *Asianweek*, 10-11.

MacManus, Susan, and Charles Bullock, III. (1993). Women and racial/ethnic minorities in mayoral and council positions. In *The Municipal Yearbook*, pp. 70-84. Washington, D.C.: International City Management Association.

Maharidge, Dale. (1996). *The Coming White Minority: California's Eruptions and America's Future.* New York: Times Books.

Marquette, Jessee F., John C. Green, and Mark J. Wattier. (1991). A general theory of voting. Paper presented at the Midwest Political Science Association Annual Meeting, Chicago.

Matthaei, Julie and Teresa Amott. (1990). Race, gender, work: The history of Asian and Asian-American women. *Race and Class* 31:61-80.

McClain, Charles J., Jr. (1994). *In Search of Equality:The Chinese Struggle against Discrimination in Nineteenth-Century America.* Berkeley: University of California Press.

Middleton, William J. (1991). The impact of party reform in California on minority political empowerment. In Byron O. Jackson and Michael B. Preston (eds.), *Racial and Ethnic Politics in California*, pp. 221-258. Berkeley: IGS Press.

Milbrath, Lester W., and Madan L. Goel. (1977). *Political Participation, 2nd Ed.* Chicago: Rand McNally.

Miller, Arthur H., Patricia Gurin, Gerald Gurin, and Oksana Malanchuk. (1981). Group consciousness and political participation. *American Journal of Political Science* 25:494-511.

Min, Pyong Gap. (1995). Korean Americans. In Pyong Gap Min (ed.), *Asian Americans: Contemporary Trends and Issues,* pp. 199-231. Thousand Oaks, CA: Sage.

Muratsuchi, Alberrt Y. (1991). Voter registration in Asian and Pacific Islander communities: An agenda for the 1990s. *Asian American Policy Review* 2:17-31.

Nakanishi, Don T. (1986a). Asian American politics: An agenda for research. *Amerasia Journal* 12(2):1-27.

Nakanishi, Don T. (1986b). "The UCLA Asian Pacific American Voter Registration Study." Los Angeles: Asian Pacific American Legal Center.

Nakanishi, Don T. (1991). The next swing vote? Asian Pacific Americans and California politics. In Byran O. Jackson and Michael B. Preston (eds.), *Racial and Ethnic Politics in California*, pp. 25-54. Berkeley: IGS Press.

Nakanishi, Don T. (1996). The growing impact of Asian Pacific Americans in American politics. In James Lai (ed.), *National Asian Pacific American Political Almanac, 7th Ed.*, pp. 7- 9. UCLA Asian American Studies Center.

Nakanishi, Don T. (1997). When numbers do not add up: Asian Pacific Americans and California politics. In Michael B. Preston and Sandra Bass (eds.), *Racial and Ethnic Politics in California, 2nd Ed.* Berkeley: IGS Press.

Nelson, Dale C. (1979). Ethnicity and socioeconomic status as sources of participation. *American Political Science Review* 73:1024-1038.

O'Hare, William, and Judy C. Felt. (1991). *Asian Americans: America's Fastest Growing Minority Group.* Washington, D.C.: Population Reference Bureau, Inc.

Okihiro, Gary Y. (1994). *Margins and Mainstreams: Asians in American History and Culture.* Seattle: University of Washington Press.

Omatsu, Glenn. (1990). Movement and process: Building campaigns for mass empowerment. *Amerasia Journal* 16(1):63-80.

Omi, Michael, and Howard Winant. (1986). *Racial Formation in the United States.* NY: Routledge.

Ong, Paul, and Tania Azores. (1994). Asian Immigrants in Los Angeles: Diversity and Divisions. In Paul Ong, Edna Bonacich, and Lucie Chenget,(eds.), *The New Asian Immigration in Los Angeles and Global Restructuring*, pp. 100-129. Philadelphia: Temple University Press.

Ong, Paul, and Suzanne Hee. (1993). The growth of the Asian Pacific American population: Twenty million in 2020. In *The State of Asian Pacific America: Policy Issues to the Year 2020*, pp. 11-24. Los Angeles: LEAP Asian Pacific American Public Policy Institute and UCLA Asian American Studies Center.

Ong, Paul, and Suzanne Hee. (1994). Economic diversity. In *The State of Asian Pacific America: Economic Diversity, Issues and Policies*, pp. 31-56. Los Angeles: LEAP Asian Pacific American Public Policy Institute and UCLA Asian American Studies Center.

Ong, Paul, and Don Nakanishi. (1996). Becoming Citizens, Becoming Voters: The Naturalization and Political Participation of Asian Pacific Immigrants. In Bill Ong Hing and Ronald Lee (eds.), *Reframing the Immigration Debate*, pp. 275-305. Los Angeles: LEAP Asian Pacific American Public Policy Institute and UCLA Asian American Studies Center.

Ong, Paul, Edna Bonacich, and Lucie Cheng. (Eds.) (1994). *The New Asian Immigration in Los Angeles and Global Restructuring.* Philadelphia: Temple University Press.

Ong, Paul, Yen Espiritu, and Tania Azores. (1991). "Redistricting and Political Empowerment of Asian Pacific Americans in Los Angeles: A Position Paper." Los Angeles: LEAP Asian Pacific American Public Policy Institute and UCLA Asian American Studies Center.

Osajima, Keith. (1988). Asian Americans as the model minority: An analysis of the popular press image in the 1960s and 1980s. In Okihiro, Gary Y., Hune, Shirley, Hansen, Arthur A., and Liu, John M. (Eds.) *Reflections on Shattered Windows: Promises and Prospects for Asian American Studies*, pp. 165-174. Pullman, WA: Washington State University Press.

Pachon, Harry. (1985). Political mobilization in the Mexican-American community. In Walker Connor (ed.), *Mexican-Americans in Comparative Perspective*, pp. 245- 256. Washington, DC: Urban Institute.

Pachon, Harry. (1991). U.S. citizenship and Latino participation in California politics. In Byran O. Jackson and Michael B. Preston (eds.), *Racial and Ethnic Politics in California*, pp. 71-88. Berkeley: IGS Press.

Padilla, Felix M. (1985). On the nature of Latino ethnicity. In Rodolfo de la Garza et al. (eds.), *The Mexican-American Experience*, pp. 332-345. Austin: University of Texas Press.

Pardo, Mary. (1990). Mexican American women grassroots community activists: "Mothers of East Los Angeles." *Frontiers* 11:1-7.

Parenti, Michael. (1967). Ethnic politics and the persistence of ethnic identification. *American Political Science Review* 61:717-726.

Parrillo, Vincent. (1982). Asian Americans in American politics. In Joseph Roucek and Bernard Eisenberg (eds.), *America's Ethnic Politics*. pp. 89-111. Westport, CT: Greenwood Press.

Patterson, Orlando. (1975). Context and choice in ethnic allegiance: A theoretical framework and Caribbean case study. In Nathan Glazer and Daniel Moynihan (eds.), *Ethnicity*, pp. 305-349. Cambridge, MA: Harvard University Press.

Patterson, Samuel C., and Gregory A. Caldeira. (1983). Getting out the vote: Participation in gubernatorial elections. *American Political Science Review* 77:675-689.

Petrocik, John R., and Daron Shaw. (1991). Nonvoting in America: Attitudes in context. In William Crotty (ed.), *Political Participation and American Democracy*, pp. 67- 88. Westport, CT: Greenwood Press.

Pomper, Gerald. (1980). The contribution of political parties to American democracy. In Gerald Pomper (ed.), *Party Renewal in America*, pp. 1-17. New York: Praeger.

Portes, Alejandro, and Rafael Mozo. (1985). Political adaptation process of Cubans and other ethnic minorities in the United States: A preliminary analysis. *International Migration Review* 19:35-63.

Portes, Alejandro, and Ruben Rumbaut. (1990). *Immigrant America: A Portrait.* Berkeley: University of California Press.

Presser, Stanley, Michael Traugott, and Sandra Traugott. (1990). Voter "over" reporting in surveys: The records or the respondents. Paper presented at the International Conference on Measurement Errors, Tucson.

Ragsdale, Lyn, and Jerrold G. Rusk. (1993). Who are nonvoters? Profiles from the 1990 Senate elections. *American Journal of Political Science* 37:721-746.

Reimers, David M. (1992). *Still The Golden Door: The Third World Comes To America, 2nd Ed.* New York: Columbia University Press.

Riggins, Stephen H. (1992). The promise and limits of ethnic minority media. In Stephen Riggins (ed.), *Ethnic Minority Media*, pp. 276-287. Newbury Park, CA: Sage.

Roosens, Eugene E. (1989). *Creating Ethnicity: The Progress of Ethnogenesis.* Newbury Park, CA: Sage.

Rosenstone, Steven J., and John M. Hansen. (1993). *Mobilization, Participation, and Democracy in America.* New York: Macmillan.

Rosenstone, Steven J., and Raymond E. Wolfinger. (1978). The effect of registration laws on voter turnout. *American Political Science Review* 72:22-45.

Rothenberg, Stuart. (1989, September 15). The invisible success story. *National Review*: 43-46.

Saito, Leland Tadaji. (1992). "Politics in a New Demographic Era: Asian Americans in Monterey Park, California." Ph.D. Dissertation, University of California, Los Angeles.

Salyer, Lucy E. (1995). *Laws Harsh as Tigers: Chinese Immigrants and the Shaping of Modern Immigration Law.* Chapel Hill, NC: University of North Carolina Press.

Sandmeyer, Elmer C. (1939). *The Anti-Chinese Movement in California.* Urbana, IL: University of Illinois Press.

Sarna, Jonathan D. (1978). From immigrants to ethnics: Toward a new theory of "ethnicization." *Ethnicity* 5:370-378.

Saxton, Alexander. (1971). *The Indispensable Enemy: Labor and the Anti-Chinese Movement in California.* Berkeley, CA: University of California Press.

Schmidt, Ronald J. (1992). The political incorporation of immigrants in California: An institutional assessment. Paper presented at the Annual Meeting of the American Political Science Association, Chicago.

Shaffer, Stephen. (1982). Policy differences between voters and non-voters in American elections. *Western Political Quarterly* 35:496-510.

Shinagawa, Larry. (1995). "Asian Pacific American Electoral Participation Three Region Study: A Study of the Exit Poll and Survey Results of the November 8, 1994 Elections for the San Francisco Bay Area, New York City, and Los Angeles." Washington, DC: National Asian Pacific American Legal Consortium.

Shingles, Richard D. (1981). Black consciousness and political participation: The missing link. *American Political Science Review* 75:76-91.

Skelton, George. (1993, August 19). Voters of Asian heritage slow to claim voice. *Los Angeles Times*, A3.

Squire, Peverill, Raymond Wolfinger, and David Glass. (1987). Residential Mobility and Voter Turnout. *American Political* Science Review 81:45-65.

Sue, Stanley, and Sumie Okazaki. (1990). Asian-American educational achievements: A phenomenon in search of an explanation. *American Psychologist* 45:913-920.

Sue, Stanley, and Derald Sue. (1971). Chinese American personality and mental health. *Amerasia* 1(1):36-49.

Suzuki, Bob H. (1977). Education and the socialization of Asian Americans: A revisionist analysis of the "model minority" thesis. *Amerasia* 4(2):23-51.

Syer, John C., and John H. Culver. (1992). *Power and Politics in* California, *4th Ed.* New York: Macmillan Publishing Co.

Tachibana, Judy. (1986, November). California's Asians: Power from a growing population. *California Journal*, 535- 543.

Takagi, Dana. (1992). *The Retreat from Race: Asian-American Admissions and Racial Politics.* New Brunswick, NJ: Rutgers University Press.

Takaki, Ronald. (1989). *Strangers from a Different Shore.* Boston: Little, Brown.

Tam, Wendy. (1995). Asians—A monolithic voting bloc? *Political Behavior* 17:223-249.

Tate, Katherine. (1993). *From Protest to Politics: The New Black Voters in American Elections.* New York: Harvard University Press.

Teixeira, Ruy A. (1992). *The Disappearing American Voter.* Washington, DC: Brookings.

Torres, Rodolfo D., and ChorSwang Ngin. (1995). Racialized boundaries, class relations,and cultural politics: The Asian American and Latino experience. In Antonia Darder (ed.), *Culture and Difference*, pp. 55-69. Westport, CT: Bergin and Garvey.

U.S. Bureau of the Census. (1988). *1987 Census of Governments: Popularly Elected Officials in 1987.* Washington, D.C.: U.S. Government Printing Office.

U.S. Bureau of the Census. (1990). *Studies in the Measurement of Voter Turnout.* Current Population Reports, Population Characteristics Series P-23 No. 168. Washington, D.C.: U.S. Government Printing Office.

U.S. Bureau of the Census. (1993a). *1990 Census of Population: The Foreign-born Population in the United States.* Washington, D.C.: U.S. Government Printing Office.

U.S. Bureau of the Census. (1993b). *1990 Census of Population: Social and Economic Characteristics.* Washington, D.C.: U.S. Government Printing Office.

U.S. Bureau of the Census. (1993c). *1990 Census of Population: Social and Economic Characteristics, California.* Washington, D.C.: U.S. Government Printing Office.

U.S. Bureau of the Census. (1995a). *Statistical Brief: The Nation's Asian and Pacific Islander Population—1994.* Washington, D.C.: U.S. Department of Commerce.

U.S. Bureau of the Census. (1995b). *1992 Census of Governments: Popularly Elected Officials.* GC92(1)-2. Washington, D.C.: U.S. Government Printing Office.

U.S. Bureau of the Census. (1997). *U.S. Population Estimates by Age, Sex, Race, and Hispanic Origin: 1990 to 1996.* Washington, D.C.: U.S. Government Printing Office.

U.S. Commission on Civil Rights. (1992). *Civil Rights Issues Facing Asian Americans in the 1990s.* Washington, D.C.: U.S. Government Printing Office.

Uhlaner, Carole J. (1986). Political participation, rational actors, and rationality: A new approach. *Political Psychology* 7:551-573.

Uhlaner, Carole J. (1989). Rational turnout: The neglected role of groups. *American Journal of Political Science* 33:390-422.

Uhlaner, Carole J. (1991). Political participation and discrimination: A comparative analysis of Asians, Blacks, and Latinos. In William Crotty (ed.), *Political Participation and America Democracy,* pp. 139-170. Westport, CT: Greenwood.

Uhlaner, Carole J., Bruce E. Cain, and D. Roderick Kiewiet. (1989). Political participation of ethnic minorities in the 1980s. *Political Behavior* 11:195-232.

Umemoto, Karen. (1989). "On strike!" San Francisco State College strike, 1968-69:The role of Asian American students. *Amerasia Journal* 15(1):3-41.

Verba, Sidney, and Norman H. Nie. (1972). *Participation in America.* New York: Harper & Row.

Verba, Sidney, Norman H. Nie, and Jae-on Kim. (1978). *Participation and Political Equality: A Seven-Nation Comparison.* New York: Cambridge University Press.

Verba, Sidney, Kay Schlozman, Henry Brady, and Norman Nie. (1993a). Citizen activity: Who participates? What do they say? *American Political Science Review* 87:303-318.

Verba, Sidney, Kay Schlozman, Henry Brady, and Norman Nie. (1993b). Race, ethnicity and political resources: Participation in the United States. *British Journal of Political Science* 23:453-497.

Wang, L. Ling-chi. (1991). The politics of ethnic identity and empowerment: The Asian American community since the 1960s. *Asian American Policy Review* 2:43-56.

Waters, M. C. (1990). *Ethnic Options: Choosing Identities in America.* Berkeley: University of California Press.

Williams, J. Allen, Jr., and Suzanne Ortega. (1990). Dimensions of ethnic assimilation: An empirical appraisal of Gordon's typology. *Social Science Quarterly* 71:697- 710.

Wei, William. (1993). *The Asian American Movement*. Philadelphia: Temple University Press.

Wolfinger, Raymond E., and Steven J. Rosenstone. (1980). *Who Votes?* New Haven: Yale University Press.

Wong, Bernard P. (1982). *Chinatown: Economic Adaptation and Ethnic Identity of the Chinese*. Fort Worth, TX: Holt, Rinehart and Winston, Inc.

Wu, Frank. (1997a, February-March). Damned if we don't. *A. Magazine*, 56-60.

Wu, Frank. (1997b, March 7). Fundraising investigation targets Asian Pacific Americans. *Asianweek*, 8-10.

Wu, Frank. (1997c, March 21). Magazine cover revives old caricatures. *Asianweek*, 8, 10.

Yancey, William, Eugene Ericksen, and Richard Juliani. (1976). Emergent ethnicity: A review and reformulation. *American Sociological Review* 41:391-403.

Yinger, J. Milton. (1985). Assimilation in the United States: The Mexican-Americans. In Walker Connor (ed.), *Mexican-Americans in Comparative Perspective*, pp. 29-55. Washington, DC: Urban Institute.

Yu, Eui-Young. (1982). Koreans in Los Angeles: Size, distribution, and composition. In Eui-Young Yu, Earl Phillips, and Eun Sik Yang, (eds.), *Koreans in Los Angeles: Prospects and Promises*. Los Angeles: Koryo Research Institute.

Index

105th Congress, 6
Abeyta, Cara J., 25, 162
Abramson, Paul R., 17, 157
Acculturation, 24, 26, 35,
  53-58, 60, 67, 69-72,
  78-80, 93, 98-103,
  106, 135, 136, 148
Affirmative action, 111, 123,
  126
African Americans. *See* blacks
Age, 8, 13, 27, 31, 32, 40, 44,
  45, 48, 52, 64, 68,
  70-73, 77-86, 88, 89,
  91, 92, 97, 99,
  102-107, 113, 114,
  116, 117, 126, 129,
  131, 139-143, 146
Aguilar-San Juan, Karen, 45,
  157, 158
Almaguer, Tomas, 5, 157
Amerasia Journal, 25, 45, 136
American Indians, 7
Amott, Teresa, 33, 164
Ancheta, Angelo N., 11, 157
Antimiscegenation laws, 35
Appointed officials, 5, 7, 9
Asian American Labor
  Alliance, 134

Asian American Movement,
  11, 15, 134, 136, 138
Asian American Political
  Alliance, 25
Asian American Republican
  Association, 133
Asian American Studies, 25,
  44
Asian Indians, 8, 9, 13, 36
Assimilation, 23-25, 32, 52,
  60, 99, 131
Asylum hearing, 111, 112,
  117-8, 120-1, 123,
  150
Attitudinal reception, 52, 53

Babbie, Earl, 47, 157
Bai, Su S., 11, 157
Barkan, Elliott R., 6, 36, 157
Barth, Fredrick, 22, 157
Baxter, Sandra, 33, 157
Behavioral reception, 52
Bennett, Claudete, 4, 18, 19,
  33, 157
Bennett, Stephen, 109, 113,
  116, 157
Berelson, Bernard R., 110, 157

For Product Safety Concerns and Information please contact our EU
representative GPSR@taylorandfrancis.com
Taylor & Francis Verlag GmbH, Kaufingerstraße 24, 80331 München, Germany

www.ingramcontent.com/pod-product-compliance
Lightning Source LLC
Chambersburg PA
CBHW050711280326
41926CB00088B/2930